Jesse Vail
North Central Hall
Naperville, Ill

SLOT T
FOOTBALL

SLOT T FOOTBALL

MAX R. SPILSBURY
Head Football Coach
Arizona State College
Flagstaff, Arizona

PRENTICE-HALL, INC., Englewood Cliffs, N.J.

PRINTED IN THE UNITED STATES OF AMERICA

81310—BC

Dedication

To the finest man it has ever been my privilege to know; a man who has always been a constant source of inspiration to me, who has dedicated his life to bringing out the very best in every boy, who has always championed the real, the good, the gentleman; a man who inspires men and boys alike to do better than they can—MR. WALDO M. DICUS, my high school coach and dearest friend.

Acknowledgments

M any thanks to the following people who in so many ways contributed to the writing of this book:

To my wife Virginia, and my five wonderful children, Kellie, Klint, Kris, Karlie, and Kennie, for all the help they give me by just being mine.

To Rose and Lou Pavlovich, of the *Tucson Daily Citizen,* without whose help I could not have written this book, for their many years of support and friendship.

To Mr. Norman Borg, our publicity man at Arizona State College, for all his many helpful suggestions.

To Art Luppino, John Lowry, Cecil Nelson, and Ted Sorich for their fine help while acting as my coaches.

To all the men who have played for me over the years at Globe High, Bisbee High, U. of Arizona, and Arizona State College.

To all the members of the Athletic Department at ASC for all the encouragement they have given me in writing this book. And to the many others who have helped to make this book a reality.

Preface

It has long been noted by those connected with professional football that the large colleges and universities have no monopoly in the development of outstanding football players. The roster of every team in the National Football League bears witness to the fine coaching of players in the so-called small colleges—men who have gone on to become professional stars. Such development is no accident, but rather the result of fine coaching and leadership on the part of dedicated coaches who work quietly and effectively far removed from the glare of the national spotlight.

Such a man is Max Spilsbury of Arizona State College of Flagstaff, Arizona. I have known Max for many years and I have watched his teams play. He is a man who brings imagination, good organization, and a challenging leadership to his approach to the game of football. His teams are interesting to watch and his players take unusual pride in achievement.

Anything, therefore, that Max Spilsbury has to say on the subject of football, technical and otherwise, is well worth the close attention of his fellow coaches, players, fans and all who enjoy our greatest collegiate game. I am confident that everyone will find something of interest in Coach Spilsbury's book on the Slot T.

LYNN O. "PAPPY" WALDORF
Director of Personnel
San Francisco Forty-Niners

Introduction

What does a football coach remember most vividly over the years? His undefeated seasons? His super stars? The electrifying 95-yard touchdown runs?

Not me.

Indelibly stamped on my memory is the sight of one of my players on the receiving end of the most vicious block I have ever seen. I still shudder when I recall it. Yet, strange as it may seem, it is a moment that I like to relive.

After being all but annihilated, the player lay still on the grass. Naturally, a substitute was rushed in. My heart was in my throat, for it appeared that the boy could have been seriously injured. He finally staggered to his feet and made his way, unaided, to the sidelines.

"Did you see that guy hit me, coach?" he asked, still trying to get his eyes in focus. "I nearly killed him!"

This scene—Arizona State vs. Chico State (California), 1958—symbolizes our team's spirit more than anything I can put my finger on. Under the most adverse conditions, this player still had the winning spirit. Despite his getting clobbered, he was still king in his own mind.

It wasn't difficult to understand why we went undefeated that season. That, in a nutshell, was the attitude of the entire team. They were tigers on an all-out football binge—which, I insist, is the only way to play the game.

Many fans and fellow coaches believe that success lies strictly on the victory side of the ledger. I say there is much more than that, including the moral and academic aspects involved. Victories are important, certainly. That is why someone invented a method of keeping score. But we stress the other values just as much as we do the victory angle.

Pride in belonging to and representing a school is of tremendous importance. We are fortunate at Arizona State College. This is an easy relationship to develop. We have a sincere, friendly faculty who will do everything in their power to help the players. If our athletes show an interest, there is not a member of the faculty who will not go more than half-way to help a youngster.

After a year with the Lumberjacks, a player has developed great team pride. He likes being associated with such a wonderful group of young men. He is proud to represent his college on the playing field. He is determined not to do anything that will reflect unfavorably on his school or his teammates. He is serious about this outlook.

There are many ingredients that go into the mixture that makes for success. Each person has in his mind the ingredients that he feels are essential to his success. As he goes through life, he finds that he adds an ingredient here, cancels one there.

Those ingredients that make up the formula we have found successful are included in this book.

MAX R. SPILSBURY

Contents

SLOT T FOOTBALL

CHAPTER ONE

What Is the Slot T?

The Arizona State Slot T, a system of football used by an increasing number of coaches, is capable of being adopted at almost any level of play: It is very workable even on the high school level, where the coach is not gifted with outstanding performers in each position. This system presents a more difficult type of attack for the defense to cope with. At first glance it may appear to be only a passing formation, but it is actually quite versatile.

The Slot T is set up in the following manner: As far as the center, guards, and tackles are concerned, it is exactly like the conventional T formation. It is also alike with respect to the fullback, quarterback, and one halfback. The main difference is that the ends are spread about ten or twelve yards out, and one back—called the slotback—is placed in between the offensive tackle and one of these wide ends. He is as much an end as a back. From this man in the "slot" comes the name of the formation.

This system is one of the easiest to teach and one of the easiest to learn in football today—and the position and spacing of the backs and three wide ends make it one of the most interesting of all offenses to work with.

Some of the plays that evolve from the Slot T seem to be more effective than from a conventional T. The passes, for example, are easier to complete, due to the spread of the defense.

1

Moreover, it is not necessary to have as many great running backs as on a Tight T formation. If we have one exceptional runner on a small-college team, we are fortunate; if we have two, we are blessed indeed.

With our system, we have had good luck with one good runner, and when we have had two we have been very tough to beat. This is because the spread formation gives a good running back more room in which to show his abilities. Since the defensive men are naturally farther apart, he is able to get more yardage than when the defense is tighter and congested.

From this system the quarterback can easily adjust his offensive backfield personnel to present any one of three different formations, as shown in Diagrams 1, 2, and 3.

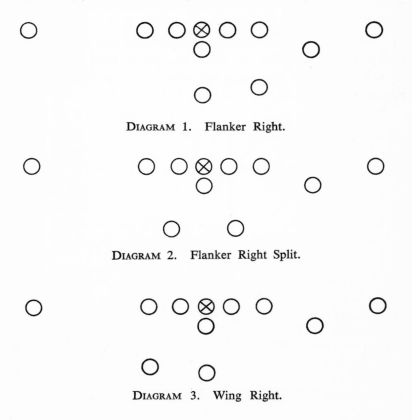

DIAGRAM 1.   Flanker Right.

DIAGRAM 2.   Flanker Right Split.

DIAGRAM 3.   Wing Right.

THE EVOLUTION OF OUR SLOT T

In 1952, while coaching at Bisbee (Arizona) High School, I first started to work with some of the ideas of the Slot T formation and its close relatives. The players I had inherited were mediocre and didn't seem to fit well into any formation. We tried them all, too—Single Wing, Split T, Straight T, and some others.

Desperately trying to find some way to move the ball, we accidentally stumbled onto a close relative of our present formation one day in practice. We were toying with a formation in which one end was spread wide, with two halfbacks lined up in the slot between our tackle and end, and we found that we could move the ball quite well.

Later, when I read Mr. Hampton Pool's fine book, *Fly T Football*,* I found that my plans and ideas fitted in well with some of his. From this came our present version of the Slot T. Diagram 4 shows our first version of the Slot T.

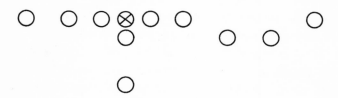

DIAGRAM 4.   Slot T Formation.

WHY THE SLOT T?

After several years of coaching experience, I have found that we have been able to score more from farther out with our Slot T than we ever could from the conventional Tight T formation.

In my first year as a college coach we stuck fairly close to

* Englewood Cliffs, N.J.: Prentice-Hall, Inc., 1960.

the Straight T. We found at the end of that season that we had scored only six touchdowns from farther out than ten yards. This meant that our offense must have been dull, uninteresting—and ineffective. After studying our game movies more times than I care to remember, we found what we thought was the trouble: Our linemen and ends were not getting the job done downfield. The blocking wasn't there. This was of concern, because our boys have always been aggressive.

In the movies we watched time after time as our eager, aggressive boys hustled downfield, trying with all their power to get the job done on the secondary backs. In the ten movies that we studied, only four or five good blocks per game were made downfield by our ends. Such blocks as the rolling cross-body block usually left our boys sprawled flat on their bellies. The roll-up block usually left them in the same position.

We finally decided that perhaps if we moved our ends out wide, we could force at least two of the defensive backs to widen out with them. These wide defensive backs, we theorized, must stay wide if our ends go downfield and turn out; they must respect this maneuver by the ends, because they never know when a fake run will be followed by a pass to one of the wide ends if they get careless. This maneuver is as good as a perfect block being executed by our ends. If a defensive back is forced wide by the maneuver of the offensive end, he is just as unable to get in on the tackle as if he had been blocked out of the play.

When the defensive backs have the ends to worry about, we can rush off tackle much stronger. Our dive plays work better, too. And if a back ever breaks through the line, his chances of making a nice gain are better without the halfbacks plugging the holes.

The wide end is not only a possible pass-receiver—he also has a beautiful angle from which to block on end-runs to his side of the line.

The more we use this type of offense, the more versatile becomes our attack. It is possible to run almost anything from this formation that can be run from any other T formation: We rush from it, pass from it, quick-kick from it. For these reasons, we are sold on the Slot T at Arizona State College.

NUMBERING SYSTEM

Our backs are numbered as follows:

Quarterback: number one back
Halfback: number two back
Fullback: number three back
Slotback: number four back

The halfback will line up in one of the dive positions, depending on the formation that has been called in the huddle, about three and a half yards behind one of the tackles. The fullback is about four yards deep and will either be directly behind the quarterback or in one of the dive positions if split formation is called. The slotback is stationed approximately four yards outside the tackle; which side he lines up on will depend on the play.

We have only three backs in our backfield—quarterback, halfback, and fullback. The slotback is as much an end as back. It is possible, however, to include the slotback in many of our backfield patterns.

The holes through which we run our plays are numbered off the hip of the offensive linemen. We give the holes to the right of the center even numbers; the holes to the left of the center odd numbers, starting from the center and working out in both directions. Off the right hip of the center is the zero hole. Off the right hip of the right guard is the two hole. Off the right hip of the right tackle is the four hole. Off the right hip of the slotback, when he is lined up on the right side, is the six hole. Around right end is the eight hole. Occasionally the wide end is brought into a tight formation when he is on the opposite side of the line from the slotback. In these plays, the hole off his hip is numbered the same as if he were the slotback.

Off the center's left hip is the one hole. Off the left guard's
left hip is the three hole. Off the left tackle's left hip is the five
hole. Off the slotback's or the tight end's left hip is the seven hole.
Around left end is the nine hole (see DIAGRAM 5).

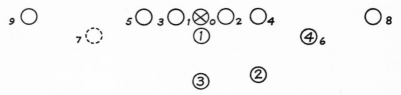

DIAGRAM 5.   Slot T Numbering System.

I believe most coaches use a similar numbering system. It is
easy to teach and easy for even the inexperienced boy to understand. No matter what offensive formation the quarterback
wishes his team to assume at the line of scrimmage, he calls one
number to let the backs know who will carry the ball, another
to designate the hole at which the play is aimed. If the two back
hears his number called first, he understands that he will carry
the ball; when he hears the next number called he knows which
hole he will hit.

On reverses, three numbers are called out in the huddle. The
call of two four seven, for example, tells the two back that he
will get the ball and give it to the number four back, who will
run through the seven hole.

SUMMARY

The Slot T is an offensive formation spread out in such a way
that no more than two good running backs are needed. It is
easy to move a man or two with no change in his blocking or
play assignment. This move can and usually does cause worry
to the defense. The passing threat is always present.

Our backs are numbered in such a way that no matter where
they are lined up, it is simple to get them into any pattern we
like. It is a most flexible offense.

CHAPTER TWO

Series Method of Teaching Backfield Patterns

We have tried many methods of teaching our backfield patterns to our backs. The one that has proven most successful is probably known to some readers; it will be discussed, however, for the benefit of those who are not familiar with it.

We teach our backs three basic groups of plays. The backs have only as many plays to learn as we have series. Each group is given a particular name; for example, our regular T-formation plays, such as the dive, off-tackle, and the pitch-out plays, form one group we call the Red Series.

For each series, the backs will run assigned patterns. Every time Red Series is called, it tells each back the pattern he is to run. The halfback, for example, will run through the same hole every time Red Series is called. He will carry the ball when his play in Red Series is called; on all other Red Series calls, he will fake getting the ball.

White Series is another group movement from which a different series of plays is run. The halfback's path is not the same for each White Series play—as it is in the Red Series—but the series call still helps him know what fake he will execute or through which hole he will carry the ball.

Our White Series is planned so that the halfback can run an end sweep, or fake the end sweep and hit off tackle, or fake the off-tackle play and hit off guard. Thus the halfback is aided by the fact that the three plays just mentioned are companions of each other, and he starts in the same direction on all three.

Blue Series is our third series. At the end of the explanation of each series, we will diagram each and the formation from which it is best run.

From any of the series just mentioned, it is possible for the quarterback to change the pattern of any *one* back by telling him, in so many words, to run another pattern. Even if the quarterback changes the pattern of one of the backfield men on Red Series, the other two backs will execute their assigned fakes for Red Series.

For example, if the quarterback has been using this series frequently, his fullback has been slanting off tackle on each previous Red Series play. All that is necessary to change the fullback's pattern is for the quarterback simply to tell him which new pattern he wishes him to run. He wants the defense to think that the play is hitting the same place the previous play hit, so he calls Red Series 31. This call tells the backs that they are to run their Red Series patterns, but the call 31 changes the pattern of one of the backs, the fullback. Instead of hitting the off-tackle hole as he does on all Red Series, the fullback (three back) now runs the new pattern: The quarterback's call of 31 indicates that he will carry the ball through the one hole. He fakes going off tackle, as he does on all regular Red Series plays, but after one step in that direction he cuts back through the opposite side of the line. All other backs run their regular Red Series patterns.

This will permit the quarterback to fool the defense with a Red Series fake, but have one of the backs hitting a new pattern. If he calls Red Series 38, this sends every back through his regular Red Series fake except the fullback, who hits a 38—the three back through the eight hole, as the signal for the play indicates.

This system has been helpful in teaching our plays, yet it gives the quarterback room for initiative of his own. The combination of simplicity and flexibility is poison to the opposition.

WHITE SERIES

We do not wish to run all our plays from the same backfield maneuvers. In the first place, this is rather difficult to do. On Red Series, the backs who are not carrying the ball are pretending to be. White Series sets up a different set of patterns.

This series includes our power-type plays: The two-time block is usually employed at the hole, and inside-out blocking by one of our backs or a pulling lineman is generally utilized. The same simple terminology still applies. If White Series 28 is called, for example, "White Series" tells the backs which pattern they are to run; the number two tells the halfback (number two back) that he is the ball-carrier; and the number six tells him which hole he will carry the ball through.

We usually run five or six plays from each series. From White Series, the basic plays include the end sweep, the off-tackle power play, the trap up the center, the fake trap up the center with a pitch-out to the fullback, and the reverse with the slotback carrying the ball. Each of these plays is shown in Diagrams 6-12. (The Red Series is covered quite completely in Chapter 8, so we will not duplicate it here.)

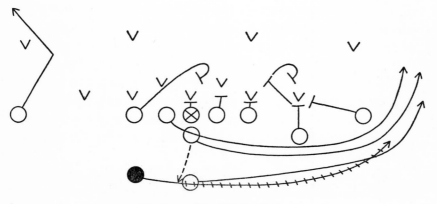

DIAGRAM 6.   White Series.

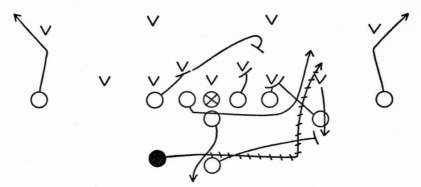

DIAGRAM 7.   Play 26 Power (White Series).

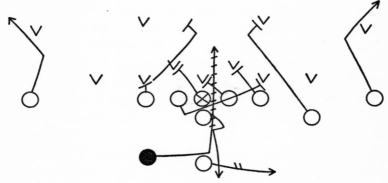

DIAGRAM 8.   Play 20 Trap (White Series).

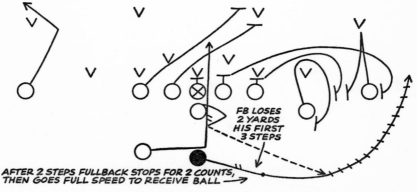

DIAGRAM 9.   Play 38 Fake 20 Trap (White Series).

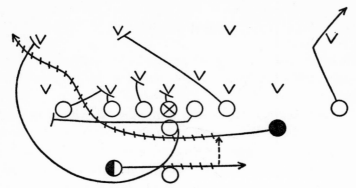

DIAGRAM 10. Play 247 (White Series).

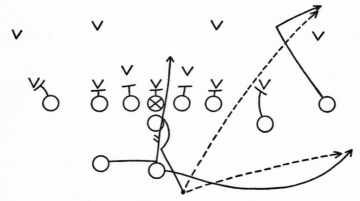

DIAGRAM 11. 20 Trap Pass (White Series).

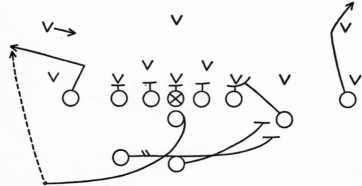

DIAGRAM 12. Fake 26 Power Check Pass to Left End (White Series).

BLUE SERIES

The third series of plays we employ is called the Blue Series. The only difference between these series is the patterns run by the backs.

The Blue Series includes the four plays shown in Diagrams 13-16. Of course, we can also run the same plays to the opposite side of the line. Blue Series is a quick-hitting series, and it can be used to get around the ends in a hurry. (This set of plays was taken from Hampton Pool's book, *Fly T Football.*) We have had varying degrees of success with this series. In some seasons it has been outstanding for us; in other years, the results have been disappointing. It is possible, of course, that it was called against the wrong type of defenses when it failed.

On Blue Series plays, the halfback swings quickly to the flat. The fullback takes a long lateral step and, with his arms folded high in front of his chest, he dives off tackle. The quarterback pitches the ball right under the fullback's folded arms, through the angle formed by his bent-over position.

If the defensive end tends to play too wide, the give to the fullback is an excellent play. The quick fake to the wide-swinging halfback and the quick trap over center have also been effective. Occasionally, the reverse trap with the slotback carrying has been a good play. These four plays to both sides make an excellent addition to our offense. This series makes the defense wide-conscious and is a good companion series for Red Series.

As in the other two series explained earlier, all the backs hit their assigned holes on each Blue Series fake. The quarterback can change the pattern of any one of the backs by calling his number through another hole. The remaining backs know where to go when they hear the series color called.

Shown in Diagrams 13-16 are the four plays that we use to both sides of the line from our Blue Series.

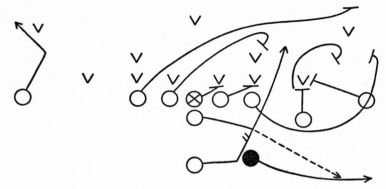

DIAGRAM 13. Play 28 (Blue Series).

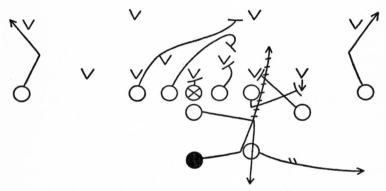

DIAGRAM 14. Play 36 (Blue Series).

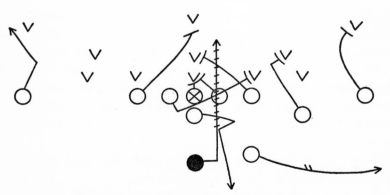

DIAGRAM 15. Play 30 Trap (Blue Series).

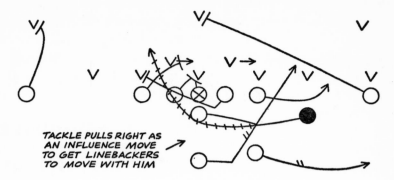

TACKLE PULLS RIGHT AS
AN INFLUENCE MOVE
TO GET LINEBACKERS
TO MOVE WITH HIM

DIAGRAM 16.   Play 41 Trap (Blue Series).

SUMMARY

Many teams use a similar method of calling their signals, but this information may help some coach find a better way of teaching plays. The series method (by which more than one play at a time can be learned) has been helpful in teaching our players the things they must learn without confusing them.

We use the three series: Red, White, and Blue. From these series many dozens of plays can be run. All that is necessary for the backs to learn is what they do when a certain series is called. Consequently, the backs must know only three or four actual plays.

Simplicity is the key to success. Plays must be simple enough for each man on the team to know them perfectly. The series method of teaching plays makes any system more simple to understand.

A team is only as sharp as its dullest player. With the series method, it is possible for every player to understand what to do and when to do it.

CHAPTER THREE

Slot T Offensive Backfield Play

The main strength of the Slot T offense is that fewer backs of great ability are required to muster a respectable offense. We have been able to move the ball considerably better with the Slot T, and one of the most important reasons is that we have been able to utilize all the talents of a small number of backs more fully. We have been able to distribute the ball-carrying chores evenly between our two finest ball-carriers.

HALFBACK

The position of halfback on our Slot T formation is a flexible one. He can hit any hole along the line from any of three or four different backfield formations. At the end of this discussion on halfbacks are diagrammed some of the plays the halfback runs. Notice that the same play is diagrammed several times, each time from a slightly different backfield formation.

These plays demonstrate how evenly the load is divided between the halfback and the fullback. At the end of the discussion on fullback will be found some of the fullback's play patterns. As the diagrams indicate, if we have two good backs we can place them in position to be of the greatest advantage on each play.

Over the years we have experimented with many formations, and we sincerely believe that the Slot T is the formation to use to get the most out of our material.

The boys that we have used at our halfback positions have varied in size, shape, color, ability, and every other way. The boys that we believe fill the halfback position best on our offense are the stocky, bulldog-built players, if you are familiar with quarter-horse talk. A shorter, heavily-muscled lad can take a lot of punishment and bounce back for more; he seems able to take a battering much better than can the tall, thinner-built boys.

STANCE

In 1957, our backfield coach was Art Luppino, a young man who had been an outstanding back for the University of Arizona, where for two seasons in succession he led the nation in rushing. He taught our backs a balanced stance. He had them place their feet almost parallel and about shoulder-width apart. He would allow a slight stagger of the feet, but not more than toe to instep. From this position, he had them squat down on their haunches and then reach forward and place their right hands on the ground. He wanted so little weight on the hand that the player could take it off the ground and not lose his balance.

From this well-balanced stance, our backs can go in any direction easily. They lose some of their straight-ahead power, but so little it is not noticeable after they learn to start well from the balanced stance. Actually, after they learn to handle the stance well, the backs can "cheat" a little and place more weight on their hands with no give-away signs.

An interesting incident convinced us that this was the best stance for our offense. In 1956, our leading ground-gainer was Cruz Salas, a 205-pounder, who used the old staggered stance. Our number two fullback was Ron Cote; Cruz could beat him around end by a full stride.

During the summer of 1957, Cote was working in town. Art got in touch with him, and together they worked on the balanced stance. When practice started in September, Cote, now using the balanced stance, could beat Salas by a full step. We think our average backs can gain a step getting around end using this balanced stance.

We use our halfback to hit every single hole along the line of scrimmage. This necessitates his being in a stance from which he can hit any hole as quickly as possible.

We use the halfback to block defensive guards, defensive ends, and defensive linebackers. In the course of a game, he will get bruised up a lot. This is why we want him to be the rugged, well-muscled type—they seem to be more durable.

RECEIVING THE BALL

Our backs have only a few things to learn about taking the ball from the quarterback. We've had little luck having our backs take the ball from the quarterback with the ball-carrier's inside arm high. This high elbow has often struck the arm of the quarterback, causing him to fumble the ball. This can also be painful to the quarterback's arm.

We have had much more success taking the ball from the quarterback in the following manner: First the back learns to take the ball from the quarterback using only his outside hand and arm. The inside arm is placed behind the runner's back. The elbow of the arm in use is placed on the outside hip and acts as a stopper for the ball. The forearm is held in a horizontal position close to the stomach, but just less than a ball's width away from the stomach. As the ball is placed in the pocket, the arm snaps tightly around it.

After this one-armed handling has been mastered, we bring in the other arm. It is held alongside and slightly back of the side of the body. The elbow of this arm is slightly crooked, so that the crook exposes more of the pocket into which the ball will be placed. As the ball is placed in the pocket, the outside elbow and forearm stop the forward progress of the ball. The outside forearm and hand trap the ball. The inside arm, hanging slightly down and back, automatically snaps up under the ball, forming a snug hold.

We have several drills that help the backs hold onto the ball. They also help the backs to hit the line low and in good running position.

One of these drills is "running the gauntlet." Two lines of backs are formed parallel to each other, facing the ball-carrier, who runs between the lines of men. They try to jerk the ball away from him. They shove him, push him, and try to knock him down. This makes the backs run properly or else get knocked from their feet.

Another drill that we use is a bit more severe, but it encourages the boys to hold onto the ball. Two linemen are placed at normal blocking distance apart. These men block the two defensive men who are head on them. A free linebacker is placed behind the line. When the back hits the line, this free agent blasts into him as hard as he can, trying to jar the ball loose. If the linebacker is successful in jarring the ball loose, the fumbling back repeats the drill three times. This particular drill is also a good tackling drill for the linebackers.

After several weeks of drills of this nature, the backs generally learn to hold onto the ball. This same type of drill is useful in helping backs learn to protect themselves when they fake into the line. They have to assume a low, hard-running form to keep the linebacker from hurting them. This tends to make the backs fake better and, at the same time, it protects them when they are tackled, if the fake is successful.

We have never been blessed with enough assistant coaches to really break the different positions down into small groups; consequently, we have not been able to teach all the fine points that the players receive at larger institutions. We try to teach the bare essentials of blocking, tackling, hard running, and faking. The things just mentioned are the ones that have helped us most.

It has long been taught by the great football men of the past and present that there is no substitute for the fundamentals of football—blocking and tackling. With this philosophy we are in complete accord.

But let's get back to the ball-carriers. Diagrams 17-27 show some of the patterns that our halfback runs from the three main offensive formations of this system of offensive football.

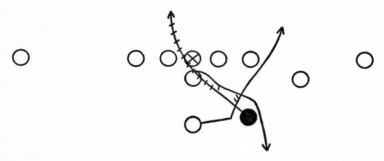

DIAGRAM 17. Flanker Right Play 21 Speed (Red Series).

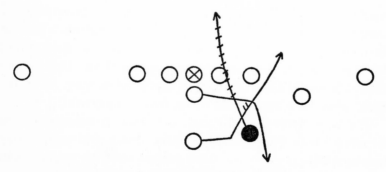

DIAGRAM 18. Flanker Right 22 (Red Series).

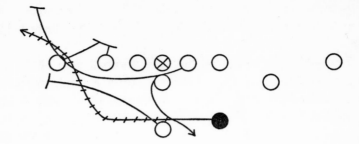

DIAGRAM 19.   Flanker Right 27 (White Series).

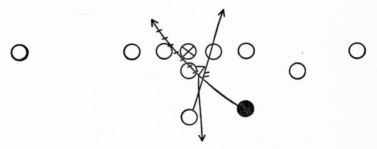

DIAGRAM 20.   Flanker Right 21 Cross Buck.

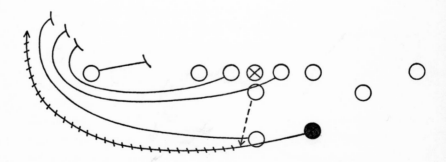

DIAGRAM 21.   Flanker Right 29 Sweep.

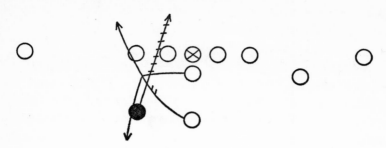

DIAGRAM 22. Wing Right 23.

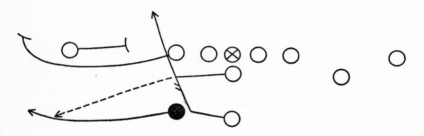

DIAGRAM 23. Wing Right 29 Pitch.

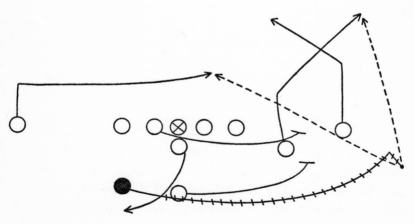

DIAGRAM 24. Wing Right 28 Pass.

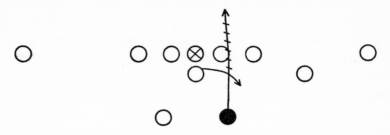

DIAGRAM 25.   Split Formation 22.

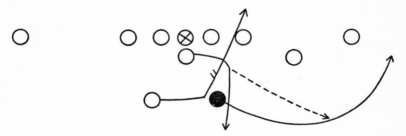

DIAGRAM 26.   Split Formation 28.

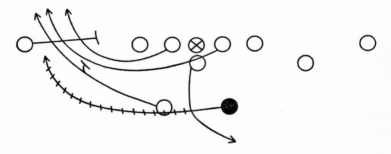

DIAGRAM 27.   Split Formation 29.

FULLBACKS

Most of what was said regarding the halfback will hold true for the fullback as well. His stance is identical. His paths into the line will be similar. He will block in the approximate same localities. He will take the ball in the same manner as does the halfback.

However, one thing that the fullback must have to play this position well is *speed*. We can get along with a halfback with only mediocre speed, but our fullback's patterns are motivated by the fact that he is our bread-and-butter player—so much so that if we do not have good speed at this position, we are in trouble. Size is not an absolute requirement. Certainly, it helps to have a big man who can move well at any position. But we have had fine success with a 145-pound boy, Bill McCormick, who could run the 100 yards in 9.7 seconds.

A fullback must be able to get around the ends and he must be able to block well on pass-protection blocking. We have found that a small boy can block the biggest ends available, if he will do it correctly. He should step up into the line and let the end go by him. As the end gets just even with him, he should simply turn and run alongside him. Then, gently placing his shoulder in the small of the end's back, he can use the end's own momentum to keep him going in the direction he is already heading. This type of block can be used effectively by very light backs versus ends twice their size.

The fullback can hit all the offensive holes along the line; consequently, he uses the same stance as the halfback. The fullback will generally carry the ball more than the halfback. His general position behind the quarterback seems to be more advantageous than the halfback's position for hitting the long-gaining holes. Our long-gaining holes have usually been our off-tackle slants and end runs. The fullback can get to them both with more speed and power from this offense than can the halfback.

Shown in diagrams 28-34 are patterns that our fullback can run from each of our three backfield formations.

SLOTBACKS

This is really a great position to play. The boys who play the slot position seem to enjoy it more than any other spot.

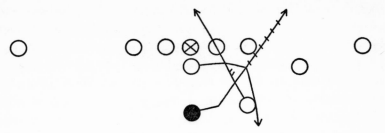

DIAGRAM 28. Flanker Right 36.

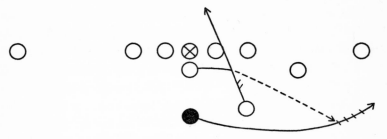

DIAGRAM 29. Flanker Right 38.

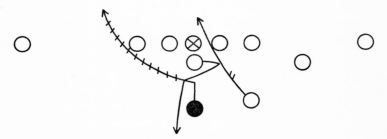

DIAGRAM 30. Flanker Right 37.

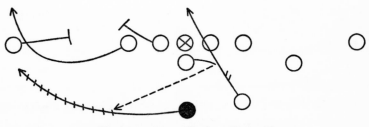

DIAGRAM 31. Flanker Right 39.

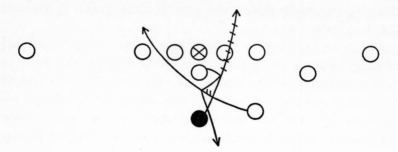

DIAGRAM 32. Flanker Right 32.

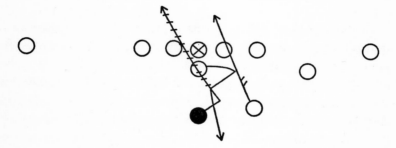

DIAGRAM 33. Flanker Right 31.

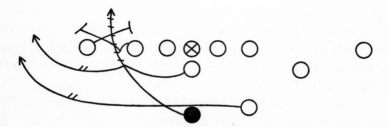

DIAGRAM 34. Flanker Right 37 Belly.

There are so many things that can be done from this position that it is really a challenge.

When we first thought of using this formation, our ends had already learned a set of rules. For this reason, we thought that we could simply move the end one yard back from the line of scrimmage and use him for a slotback. When we wanted a slotback set left, the left end would drop off the line and the wide-spread halfback would move up on the line, and vice-versa.

The ends could still use all their blocking rules, even from the slot position. They themselves felt that anything they could do from up on the line, they could do better from off the line. This worked out well for us, but it necessitated the backs' learning two sets of plays—the regular halfback plays, plus wide end plays.

In the spring of 1959, it was decided to have a permanent slotback. It was also decided to have permanent wide ends—the same boys out there all the time. They learned to do a better job of the wide end assignments. Before, when one end was used as the slotback, the other end would be spread as a wide end; he had two positions and several extra types of blocks and pass patterns to learn. The slotback also found that he could do a better job when concentrating on one position.

The slotback is lined up about a yard off the line and from one to four yards outside of the tackle, facing the area in front of the tackle. He is in a position to block the tackle or the linebacker, to come back on a reverse, or to go downfield as a blocker or pass-receiver. It seems to worry the defensive tackle to have the slotback looking right down his throat all the time, especially after he has been blocked by the slotback a few times. From his position off the line, the slotback can really be moving when he makes contact.

We like our slotbacks to be good-sized boys. They are called upon to do a lot of blocking. There are some things we can sacrifice at this position, but blocking ability is not one of them.

The slotbacks are used in many different ways. They are primarily blockers, but they receive many passes and they carry the ball on several different plays. At the end of this discussion on the slotback are shown the types of plays in which he is the ball-carrier. The speed with which he can hit several holes will surprise you.

It is difficult to find a boy to play this position who can block, run well, and at the same time be a good pass-receiver. Usually, however, it is possible to find a boy who can do two of the three of these well. Exploit his abilities, not his liabilities. If he is a good pass-receiver, pass to him. If he is a good runner, include plays on which he carries the ball. But there can be no question of his blocking; he must be able to block or he cannot play this vital position.

If the slotback is a real horse and worries the defensive tackle enough, the tackle will be outside-conscious. When the defensive tackle is worried about the slotback, he is susceptible to our inside attack. The slotback can fake him easily after he has blocked in on him a few times. He will run right at him as if to block him, then shoot past him and block the linebacker. He can do the same thing and cut back out for a pass.

The distance that the slotback positions himself away from the tackle and the line of scrimmage is never the same. He will constantly vary his position so that *where* he is will never be a key for the defense to figure out plays.

STANCE OF THE SLOTBACK

The stance of the slotback is not the same as the other two backs. It is more staggered, and more weight is placed on the hand for powerful forward thrust. He will need much straight-ahead power for his block on the tackle. When he is lined up on the right, his left hand is down and his left leg back. Why?

Because he is only asked to go in two directions—straight ahead, and back to his inside. From this position, he can go straight ahead as well as he could from his position of right hand down and right foot back, and he can go back to the inside much faster. He only has to drive off his outside leg as he reaches with his inside leg and he is immediately on his way in the desired direction.

The opposite is true when he is lined up as a slotback on the left, and for the same reasons. When he is a slot left, his right hand will be down and right leg back.

The slotback knows on which side to line up from the direction given by the quarterback. He merely listens to the direction, not the formation. The formation tells him nothing. If the signal is flanker right, the word "right" is all that matters to the slotback.

We have experimented a great deal with the slotback position. Sometimes we have placed him up on the line and used our wide end as a back. But it seems to us that he is more valuable when back off the line. It is much more difficult for the defense to keep the slotback from getting out into a pass pattern when he is lined up one or two yards off the line; he has more room in which to fake and out-maneuver the man trying to hold him up. We think the slotback is a better blocker from off the line, also. Many boys have trouble blocking a defensive man if he is not within the lunge distance of their primary block. The linebackers seem to ward off the blocker easily when he has no impetus. Back him off the line and he gets two extra steps into his block. This has proven more satisfactory for us.

From his unusual position (lined up almost in a normal backfield position, yet facing in at such an angle that the ball can be flipped to him from the quarterback), the slotback has a real advantage. He can also be brought back in motion to present other problems for the defense. Diagrams 35-40 show some of his plays.

SLOTBACK PLAYS

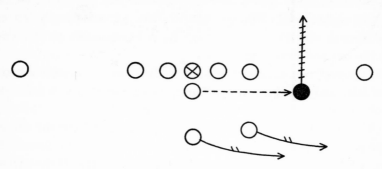

DIAGRAM 35. Flanker Right 46.

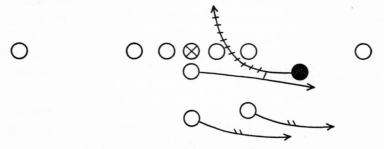

DIAGRAM 36. Flanker Right 42.

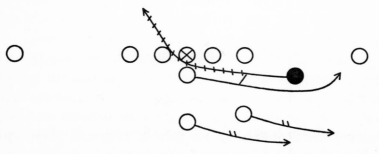

DIAGRAM 37. Flanker Right 41.

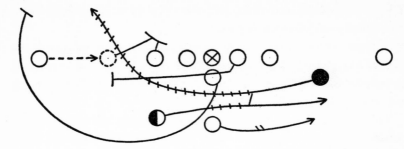

DIAGRAM 38.   Wing Right 247.

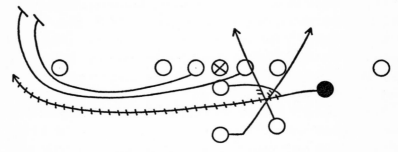

DIAGRAM 39.   Flanker Right 49.

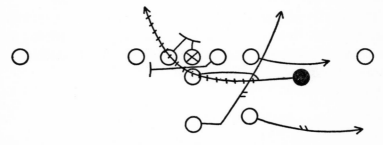

DIAGRAM 40.   Flanker Right 41 Trap.

SUMMARY

Although our backs may not have learned all the fine points
of the game, they know how to block and tackle. They know

how to fake hard and run hard, too. If they will do these well, it is usually satisfactory for us.

Players on our team enjoy themselves. Our backs especially like working with this formation. There are few set standards to adhere to. The quarterback can be flexible, and the attack is varied as necessary.

The wide ends are the "trademarks" of this formation. They can be any type, physically—tall and thin, short and fat, or a mixture of the two. Any outstanding ability they might possess can be exploited to its fullest from this position.

Our slotback must be a fine blocker, pass-receiver, and runner. He has a variety of duties to perform in each game.

Our fullbacks need not be the type generally considered necessary for this position. They can be any size, if they are fast. We can teach them to block the big, tough men in such a way that they will not be injured.

The halfback will have an opportunity to use his skills in many different ways. He will have a chance to run at all the offensive holes; surprise defensive linemen once in a while with a block instead of a fake; he will pass, be a pass-receiver, blocker, runner, and in general do a little of everything.

The Slot T quarterback faces a real challenge. Our quarterback has such freedom that he must be a bona fide thinker on the field. He will constantly strive for originality in guiding the team's offense.

CHAPTER FOUR

The Wide-Spread Ends

The position of the wide-spread end is one answer to a coach's prayer. It is possible to "hide" a player at this position. If, for example, you have a boy who is a terror on defense, but just not capable of doing much on offense, this can be the answer. With only a few plays to learn and a few blocks of any degree of difficulty to execute, this is an ideal spot.

If free substitution is used, here is the place for the speedy, skinny kid who is so fragile he may be crumpled if hit. He can be placed at this wide-end position and used only on pass patterns. This is the place to use a boy who has no size, but who can catch a pass well. A boy can be used to advantage at the wide-end position even if he does not possess enough ability to play at any other position.

Much good can come from using the players with only a limited amount of ability at this position. If there is a big, slow boy who can block well, use him at this position and let him come back down the line and block the first man to show in his direction on end-run plays. If there is a boy who starts slowly, but builds up speed as he goes, he can be placed out wide and angled across the field on look-in patterns and long look-in patterns. There may be a boy on the squad who is really a top-flight pass-receiver, but who is too slow to free himself on deep passes. He can be spread wide and used to catch hitch passes or short four-yard passes that are as effective as a dive play from the Split T.

If these things can be done with personnel of lesser ability, what can be done if you are fortunate enough to have a real prize end who can do most of the things just mentioned?

If the wide end is a great faker with speed, he can be split out so wide that the defense is forced to cover him man for man. This is a very tough assignment for a defensive halfback. Our wide ends have many patterns to run; they are discussed in the chapter on pass offense.

The wide end can work on his pass patterns and his fakes in his leisure time; if he is diligent, there are many ways in which he can improve himself. Some of our best pass-receivers come out to the field thirty minutes early every day and have one of the quarterbacks pass to them. They work on the patterns with which they can free themselves easily from different types of coverage by the defense. Some teams cover our wide ends up tight. They have a man placed right up on the line of scrimmage, and he attempts to keep our wide end from getting downfield on a pass pattern. If the wide end can become battle-tested and experienced in this type of coverage before he actually faces it in a game, he will know the weaknesses involved. He will know that it is difficult for the defense to cover our wide men tight and still be able to protect deep on passes thrown outside and behind such tight defenders.

The wide ends will be difficult to cover on look-in passes if the defense covers them either too tight or too loose. This is the pass where the wide end cuts across the field at approximately a 45-degree angle. He is free at different spots along the path of his course: He may be free as soon as he breaks in, he may be free after he runs past the first linebacker's position, or he may be free after he gets deep.

As a companion play to the look-in, we have the check-out pass. The end should work long and hard on the proper execution of this play. He must come diagonally across the field exactly as he did on the look-in. As he feels the defensive back coming close to him, he cuts sharply back toward the sideline. This maneuver is called our check pattern.

Another pattern that the end will work on during this pre- or post-practice period is our Z-in and Z-out patterns. The wide end will run eight yards, fake in, fake out, then cut back in. The Z-out pattern is just opposite. If the wide end learns to execute the hook pass, he will be able to get free on this pass any time. Our receivers have had success on the hook passes by running at the defending back, then cutting to the sideline for about three steps. As the back starts with him, the end plants his foot nearest the defensive back and cuts sharply back in the

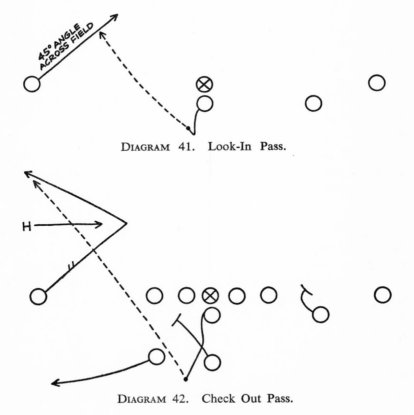

DIAGRAM 41.   Look-In Pass.

DIAGRAM 42.   Check Out Pass.

direction from which he just came. The pattern looks like a fish
hook. Diagrams 41-45 give an idea of what each of these patterns look like.

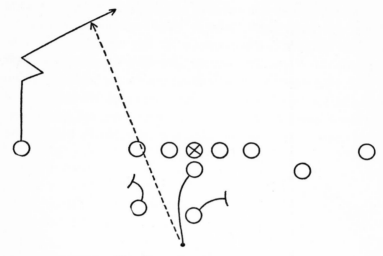

DIAGRAM 43.   Z-In-Pattern.

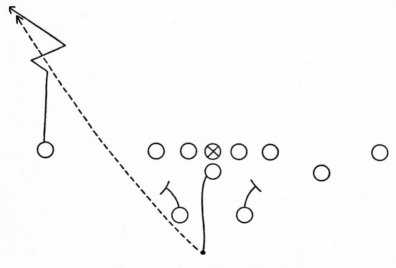

DIAGRAM 44.   Z-Out-Pattern.

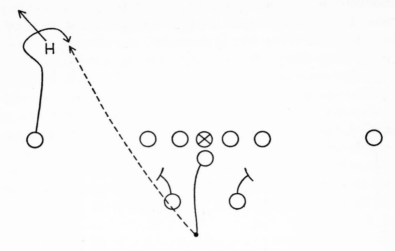

DIAGRAM 45.   Hook Pass.

STANCE OF THE WIDE END

The wide ends take a two-point stance. They stand erect with their heads turned in toward the quarterback. From this position they can come back down the line quickly and can also get into the secondary very easily.

The blocking assignments that the wide end must learn are simple. On any play coming around his side of the line, his rule is to come back down the line toward his own quarterback and block the first man that comes in his direction. If the play is an off-tackle play to his side of the line, his rule is to align himself with the hole and block through it.

On plays straight through the line or to the other side of the line, he runs a down-and-out pattern. Why? Because if he runs a down-and-out pattern, someone on defense has to see to it that he is not an intended receiver. This keeps that defender out of the play for a second or two longer. If the end is ignored on his down-and-out pattern, he can be hit with a pass for a sure touchdown when the quarterback gets the information.

Some boys will come back down the line as fast as they can run and still do a good job of blocking. Some of our boys have waited in their tracks as the defense started to drift toward them. Others have taken a step or two backwards and have waited for someone to come to them.

With this blocking rule, a stunting defense makes no difference. Someone will have to be covering the wide threat. It will be either the end or a linebacker. The wide end just waits until he sees who is coming the fastest to cover wide. This is the man he cuts down. Turning the corner is made easier if the wide end cuts the wide pursuit off as soon as possible. To do this, the end must hurry down the line quickly.

SUMMARY

The finest thing about the wide-spread end on the Slot T offense is that a very talented boy can be hidden at this position.

A boy of just about any size, shape, speed, or ability can be used here. It is a wonderful place too to have a good pass-receiver when you need him, whether or not he can do anything else well. A big boy who can block can also be used effectively at this position whether or not he can do anything else.

CHAPTER FIVE

Interior Line Play

THE CENTER

On any type of T formation, a team is no better than its center. On him depends the start of every play. He must be able to keep a cool head under all conditions. If he panics easily, he can be responsible for losing a ballgame at any moment. If he snaps the ball before the quarterback is ready, he will undoubtedly cause a fumble. If he snaps the ball back too hard, the same thing may happen. On punts, a hard-charging middle guard can cause a nervous center to snap the ball over the kicker's head.

We have many drills in which the center really catches it from a middle guard. If he tends to panic, we will line our toughest, hardest-charging men in front of him and let them try to force him to panic. This seems to help; with this practice experience, the center is ready when a middle guard tries similar tactics in a game.

A center must be able to keep a hard-charging middle guard away from the quarterback. This gives the quarterback the required amount of time necessary to execute T-formation fakes without a hitch.

A quick charge is necessary by the center on this type of formation, but he does not have to be really speedy. If he can move quickly for a short distance, he is able to do an adequate job. His blocking assignment usually pertains to a defensive man lined up head on him, or to either side of him. Occasionally he will be assigned to block a linebacker.

On plays around the ends, when the defense has no one lined up head on the center, he will block the onside halfback. We work hard, trying to get the timing on this play down to a fine point. If the center times his move just right, he will be in position to knock the halfback off the ball-carrier just as he starts to make the tackle.

We have been more successful having our offside downfield blockers sprint to a position in front of the area where the ball-carrier starts downfield. From this position they are taught to block back toward the line of scrimmage. Our backs have averaged more yards per carry since we have blocked downfield in this fashion.

Linebackers and linemen who had already been blocked once or who were just standing around doing nothing, but managed to make the tackle, were the defensive men responsible for our trying this type of blocking. Many times our backs have failed to make it far enough to get downfield assistance. The hole would open up, and the wall would form downfield. The back would cut through the hole, and someone would crawl out of the woodwork to make the tackle just as it appeared our back was free. These free men on or behind the line are the men one must move to get the job done. We try to wipe out everyone for a few yards and hope the back can get a little more on his own.

Centers can drill on delivering a tremendous blow on the snap of the ball. This drill is executed in the following manner: The center will assume his offensive blocking position. He will then simulate snapping the ball. His arms will be fully extended through his legs and out behind his buttocks. From this position, he will snap his forearms to the front with a powerful motion. At the same time he snaps his body from the waist up to a standup position. This will develop powerful back and neck muscles. It also develops speed with which the offensive center can deliver a powerful blow as he snaps the ball to the quarterback. Our centers feel, after they become proficient at snapping their arms forward with a powerful thrust, that they can do the punishing instead of taking it all the time.

PRACTICE DOES PAY

Paul Hatcher, the finest offensive center it has been my pleasure to watch, drilled this way during the off season. Paul was an all-conference center for the University of Arizona for three years in succession. Many of the University's opponents found that to place a defensive man head on Hatcher was to sentence him to a merciless beating. Hatcher was quick and strong, thanks to his practice sessions.

Our center for the past few seasons has been a boy named Ernie Hansen. He is 6'4" tall and weighs 250 pounds. He was fortunate enough to spend some time one summer working out with Paul Hatcher. Paul taught him to deliver such a blow as we just mentioned. This type of offensive blow was responsible for Hansen's tremendous improvement.

Our center must be able to snap the ball at least fifteen yards deep. We use the deep punt for our spread punt formation. Our centers will take a ball to the dorm during the off season and practice snapping it in the hallway of the dormitory. Players who are interested in improving themselves will find this beneficial. To snap the ball deep, our centers—without exception—have had to rock forward a bit to get the proper snap leverage. If they are not careful, this will be a cue on which the defense will charge. The center should go ahead and rock if he must, but instead of making a rhythmic motion, he should hesitate and stagger this motion, to confuse the enemy. (See Chapter 11 on "Kicking From the Slot T.")

We make it our center's responsibility to require that the

punters, extra-point kickers, and quick-kickers receive practice in executing their specialty each evening of practice.

The center must see to it that all quarterbacks get a few exchanges from him each practice. If we are scrimmaging and forget to have the center or quarterback trade off, one of them will call for his substitute to come over and take some exchanges. This prepares each for the feel of the other and helps cut down on fumbles.

Leadership at the center position is one of the most important boosts a coach can receive. If the center will voluntarily accept these duties, so that the above-mentioned tasks are completed each day, it will be a big help to any coaching staff.

The center's stance is not as wide as that of a single-wing center. It may be a little wider than the stance of a regular T-formation center. He should be based with a natural stagger to his feet, but never more stagger than toe to heel. We personally prefer toe to instep. It is suggested that the quarterback adjust to the center's stance, rather than having the center adjust to the quarterback's stance. The center has a difficult task of blocking a hard-charging lineman. He should be helped all the way. If he is forced to raise or lower his hips, he will be less effective as a blocker.

When the center is in a comfortable stance, the quarterback moves in behind him and assumes his stance. The center is now ready to put the ball into play. His hands are on top of the ball with his thumbs together. His fingers are slightly spread and wrapped well around the ball. The center raises the near end of the ball off the ground. This gives him a good hold on the ball and places it in excellent position to snap to the quarterback. As it is snapped back to the quarterback, the forward point of the ball is snapped under and is pointing toward the quarterback when the exchange is completed. The center does not twist his hands or arms unnaturally; as they move toward the quarterback, they move in a straight, easy motion. From the exchange position of the ball, the center's arms are in a perfect position from which to be brought powerfully forward with a tremendous lifting jolt.

A coaching point that should be noted here is this: When a young man first tries this type of exchange, he is likely to push the ball too far past the quarterback's hands. The quarterback should be urged to place a great amount of up-pressure on the center's rump. If the center is unable to feel the quarterback's hands, he has no guide by which to snap the ball. It may be necessary to have an inexperienced center bend his elbows out a little; this will shorten his arms and will help at first to place the ball in the proper position.

In practice, our centers have improved their accuracy for long snaps by snapping the ball through a rubber tire swinging or hanging motionless from the goal post (see Diagram 46).

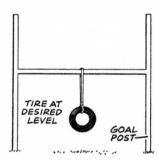

DIAGRAM 46.   Drill to Develop Accuracy for Long Snaps.

GUARD PLAY

Almost every high school in the land has one or two players between 165 and 175 pounds. Many colleges overlook these middle-sized boys. We feel that a good, rugged boy can make a good lineman, regardless of his size, within reason. The boy this size usually has a world of courage and determination. This is a characteristic that we never want to overlook. He generally makes up for his lack of size with tremendous fight.

In high school and small colleges, where the rule of free substitution is used, boys of this type are especially valuable. Our guards have been boys well under the 200-pound class for a number of years.

Lack of weight or shortness of stature does not always tell the entire story. We had a guard by the name of Frank Thomas for three years. He was 5'6" and weighed 175 pounds. We have never had any two men who could handle him. He was stronger than any man on our team and quicker than anyone we had.

Our guards pull a great deal, and they must be able to move quickly. A man does not have to be a monster to execute many types of inside-out blocks and cut-off blocks. Every coach will naturally look first for the big boy who can do all this, too. Unfortunately, we can't always get the type we want, and it is sound logic to give the middle-sized boy a chance.

Most of the smaller high school boys can move their bigger teammates all over the place. They seem to develop their muscular coordination faster. Many times this quickness is sufficient in college, too. The smaller boy who gets to the big, slow man quickly can move him or at least keep him out of the play.

Desire and ruggedness are tough to beat on any field. Our guards are called upon to move men in front of them, to block men off the line, to trap tackles, and to block ends. They must be rugged and quick.

We try never to ask more of a boy than he can give. At any hole, if the defensive man is too tough for our boy to handle, we use another plan. Our blocks, then, are planned in such a way as to be able to utilize an angle. With an angle block at their disposal, the offensive men can hit a defensive man from the front or from either side. Usually he is susceptible to one or the other of these blocks. It is usually possible to trap the boy who is really a tough straight-ahead charger. His own momentum will often carry him past the ball-carrier.

It is generally true that the tough, straight-ahead charging end is easy to get around. The same is true at any other position; it is difficult to move in one direction full speed and not be susceptible to angle blocks. The waiting type of defensive player is tougher to move most times. By trapping a hard charger with a guard, or by calling a screen pass so his hard charge will make a monkey of him, he can be slowed down. If we can slow a hard charger down, we have the advantage over him.

We have faced few defensive men who were proficient both as hard chargers and also as the waiting, hand-fighting type. This type of defense takes a great deal of time to master, and the high school and small college coach does not have the time or the help to teach this type of play.

The stance of the guard must be well-balanced, since he pulls in both directions. As close to a toe-to-toe stance as can comfortably be assumed by the guard is desirable; very little weight should be placed on the hands. Foot spread will vary with the guard's size and body build. Comfort is the first objective. As he becomes comfortable, we can improve his blocking stance as we go along.

For the straight-ahead block, the guards fire out at shoulder level without raising up one iota. Shooting forward with powerful uncoil of the legs and back, and a terrific upswing of the forearm will help greatly. This is followed by quickly bringing the legs up under the body. The shoulder and forearm should be brought up under the chest of the defensive man, lifting powerfully with arm, back, and legs.

We teach this type of block in the following manner: The blocker assumes his offensive stance, and a defensive man is moved to a head-on position over him. The defensive man is told merely to fall forward at the snap of the ball. As the ball is snapped, the offensive man uncoils and drives his shoulders into the defensive man. He brings his feet up under him and assumes a lift position. The defensive man is now hanging over the shoulder of the offensive blocker. If the offensive man can lift the defensive man off the ground, his feet are in the correct position. If he has to make an adjustment before he can lift, his feet are not in the correct position. As soon as the defensive man is hanging heavily over the offensive man's shoulder, it will be apparent whether or not he is in good position.

We correct the blocker by having him assume, slow motion, a position from which he *can* lift the defensive man. As he is able to lift the man on his shoulders, we have him stop and take careful notice of his lifting stance. He notices exactly where his feet, legs, and back are. This is the position he now knows he must assume on each block if he is to be in the correct position to lift a defensive man.

We have also taught our blockers the lunge charge. The blocker is first told to lunge into the defensive man and leave his feet planted. As he learns to blast with a strong shoulder block, we have him repeat his move, and gradually we let him bring his feet with him as he lunges. He will get his legs under him properly as he learns to lift the defensive man. The uncoil of his legs, back, and forearm are developed quickly in this way. After the blocker masters the straight-ahead charge and has his feet up under him, he is ready to do one of three things. He will block the defensive man, either to the right, left, or straight back. If he is planning to move the defensive man to the right, the blocker will bring his left leg up and outside to provide the drive force for the block in the direction desired. The opposite is true to move him to the left.

The blocker keeps contact with the defensive man with short, chopping steps. He tries to form a V with his upper arm and his head and neck. He tries to hold the defensive man in the V. If the blocker is successful in getting the defensive man into this V, he has an excellent chance of getting the job done. This same method is used to teach all linemen their blocking techniques.

The block our boys employ to hit a defensive man who is lined up in one of the gaps to either side is called a fill block.

On this assignment, the blocker steps into the man's shoulder or hip. When the defensive man is a fast charger, the blocker may have to shoot his head across in front of the defensive man. The defensive man can be rolled out of the hole if contact is made shoulder to hip, with the forearm placed across the defensive man's stomach. The hip is the heaviest part of a man, and if that portion can be rolled, the remainder of the body will necessarily follow.

There are many drills to improve the actions of linemen, but some are more effective than others. We like the drill that Crowther suggests. This is the drill where the linemen are in front of the sled on their knees. From here they lunge forward to get the idea of the use of the body and forearm. They lunge, recoil, lunge, recoil, etc.

Another drill we use a great deal is the one around the goal posts at the end zone. About a yard from the goal post, we line up all the guards and any other pulling linemen. They are about a yard outside of one of the posts, facing the end zone. On command, they go through their pulling technique. They pull and run a figure eight in and out between the two goal posts. As they round each post, they drop their inside shoulder and pull hard with their inside arm, as if banking around a tight turn. This simulates pulling up through the hole (see Diagram 47).

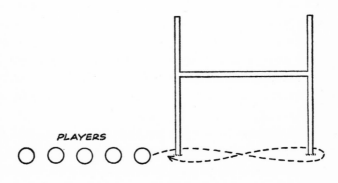

DIAGRAM 47.

TACKLE PLAY

For many years it has been our belief that in order for a team to be successful, it must be exceptionally strong in three positions: tackle, center, and quarterback. From an offensive point of view, the team's chances are excellent if these three positions are strong, even when the remaining positions are filled with mediocre personnel.

At tackle, Arizona State has been more than fortunate during the past four years to have had some of the finest tackles in the small college ranks anywhere. One tackle, Glen Morgan, was named to the first team of the NAIA All-American team—a well-deserved honor. Another tackle, Hosie Maddox, was named the outstanding lineman of the Holiday Bowl game in St. Petersburg, Florida.

Our tackles are expected to be leaders on our team. They have such a vital role to play in our plans that leadership comes to them naturally. Our offense is built around our tackles. If they fail to be leaders and "holler guys," we have trouble.

In the past we had our tackles call the offensive blocks at the line. For some tackles this worked out well, but others could not do a satisfactory job of calling offensive blocks. Some were too nervous, others too slow mentally, others simply did not understand football well enough. Now our quarterbacks call the blocking assignment with the play. The tackle is expected to advise the quarterback occasionally on the best type of block for a certain play, if the standard block for opening a specified hole is not working well. He will do this when the quarterback is standing to one side of the huddle, deciding on his next play selection.

The boy who plays tackle for us must be a good-sized boy. He is called upon to block a great deal by himself. If he can handle the defensive tackle alone, we feel our chances of winning are good. He must be fast, since he pulls and leads the end runs.

He must be able to block well downfield. He is the bread and butter of our offense.

The tackle's downfield block is executed differently from that of our other downfield blockers. We do not allow our tackle to leave his feet to execute a block. He will run right through a defensive man and try his utmost to stay on his feet. Our backs set the defensive halfbacks up for the tackle's block. The back has the responsibility of faking and maneuvering the defensive back into the path of the tackle. We try to have our tackle get around the corner as quickly as possible. He will not worry about where the defensive back is; his sole responsibility is to turn upfield quickly and stay on his feet. Our ball-carrier soon learns to get behind this man and stay there. The back will fake in and cut out or will fake out and cut back to the inside. If the back gets up close to the tackle, he will soon find that whatever move the defensive back makes is wrong. A good back will draw the defensive man right into the tackle if he fakes well.

The tackle uses the blocking form that the guards use. He will pull around end using the identical footwork used by the guards. He will have a little more stagger to his feet and a little more weight on his hand. When the tackle pulls, he will push off hard with his hand and inside leg. At the same time, his outside leg will reach, with about a six-inch step, toward the sideline. His outside arm will pull hard in a back-and-around motion. This will help him whip his body around and leave him pointing in the desired direction.

The tackle must be ready for contact on this first step. If the defensive end is crashing hard, he may bump the tackle, and a tackle who is not expecting such a move might be knocked off his feet.

If the defensive end is crashing hard, the tackle may have to step behind him and get out to the flat zone as quickly as possible. There is a useful drill that we employ to prepare the tackle. We have a linebacker, a defensive end, and a defensive halfback line up in their respective positions. As the tackle pulls in his assigned manner, any one of these three defensive men will attempt to knock him off his feet. He soon learns to dodge the first two and get to the third or the deepest one.

We always use a ball-carrier in this drill. After he has been smeared a few times, he will learn to set up the tackle's block for him.

In addition to the straight-ahead block, the tackle must learn how to post block for the slotback. On this block, the tackle comes up under the defensive tackle's chest with both forearms. This will stop the defensive man's forward progress and stand him up so the slotback has a good target. As the slotback makes contact, the tackle will swing his hips around until they touch the slotback's hips. This movement insures that they are blocking in the same direction; without it, they would be pushing against each other.

The tackle must also learn to execute the lead block for a post block by his guard. If the guard has stopped the forward progress of the defensive man, the tackle will step in with his near foot and hit with his near shoulder. His shoulder will blast into the hip of the defensive man. As the tackle makes contact, the guard will whip his hips around into the hips of the tackle, and together they will block down the line in the same direction.

One other type of block that we have our tackle learn is what we call the "quick block." On this block, our tackle will come behind his guard and shoot up through the hole on the linebacker, and the guard will shoot to his outside and block the man that is lined up on the tackle. The tackle takes a short jig step back with his inside leg. As his inside foot hits the ground, his outside leg crosses over and up through the dive hole (see Diagram 48). If the man head-on the center is sliding off the center's block, the tackle will assist the center. If the center needs no help, the tackle will shoot on through to the linebacker.

One major duty our tackles have is to captain the screen-pass team to their side of the line. They seem to take great pride in seeing that their side of the line develops into the finest organized

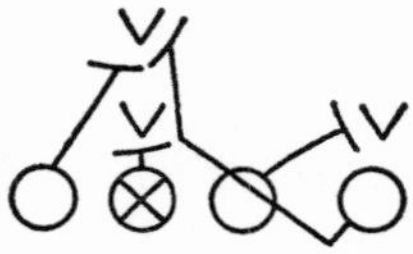

DIAGRAM 48.   Quick Block.

screen-pass unit. Friendly rivalry builds great pride, and without pride there is very little that can be accomplished.

SUMMARY

Most coaches know the type of personnel required to make their offense go. It is no different with the Slot T. We feel that we can do better with a certain type of personnel.

On the line, the centers and tackles are the real problem positions. If these spots are manned by capable men, it will be possible to get by many times with players of lesser ability at the guard and end positions, due to the type of attack we can muster from this spread-type offense.

We have found this to be advantageous in recruiting. We do not need top-caliber linemen at guard and end. This is not to say that we have not had some top performers at these spots, but when necessary we have been able to get by with men of lesser ability in these spots.

Almost every high school team has one or two middle-sized boys who are fine athletes, but who are not selected by most larger colleges. They can make fine Slot T guards. And we have had no trouble getting all the 170-pound, six-feet-tall boys we need for ends. We can use them in this type of formation, too. This use of personnel is a real advantage.

CHAPTER SIX

Slot T Blocking Rules

W e use eight different types of blocks. The linemen have these eight blocks to learn, and that is all. There are only three areas to hit on the line: the dive hole, the off-tackle hole, and the end-run area. Against an even defense there is another hole, straight up the center; we open this hole in a set way, as shown a little later in the chapter.

We open the dive hole in three different ways. We also open the off-tackle hole with three different blocks. To run the ends, we have been successful using only two different blocking techniques.

DIVE HOLE

Three methods of blocking are employed to open the dive hole:

1. Man Block (Diagram 49)
2. Quick Block (Diagram 50)
3. Trap Block (Diagram 51)

For convenience the blockers are shown against a five-man line. Our blocking rules make any type of defense as easy to attack as any other, as far as assignments are concerned.

One or the other of these three blocks will generally prove successful. We used the identical three types of blocks when I

51

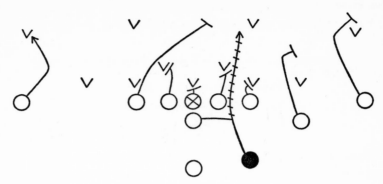

DIAGRAM 49.   Man Blocking.

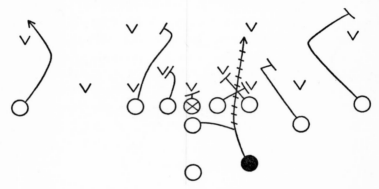

DIAGRAM 50.   Quick Blocking.

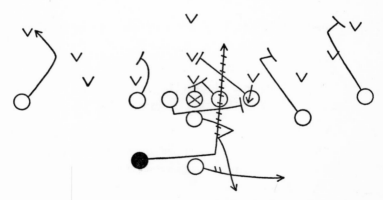

DIAGRAM 51.   Trap Blocking.

was coaching in high school. This proves that they are simple to learn, which is naturally most beneficial in college football, too.

We also open our off-tackle hole in three different ways:

1. Take Blocking (Diagram 52)
2. Spike Blocking (Diagram 53)
3. Power Blocking (Diagram 54)

These three blocks have proven to be adequate. The linemen's rules are so simple to learn that no defense that faces them is of serious worry.

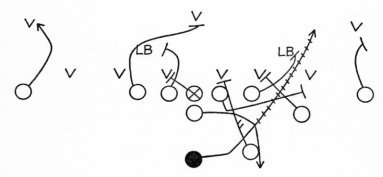

DIAGRAM 52. Take Blocking.

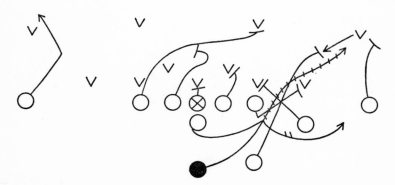

DIAGRAM 53. Spike Blocking.

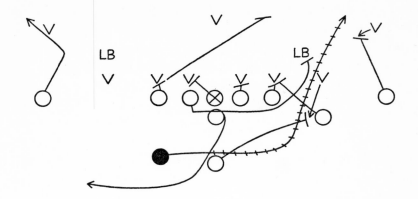

DIAGRAM 54.   Power Blocking.

We will block for the wide end run in two different ways. We have used a third method in the past, but have proven to our own satisfaction that the two methods are satisfactory. Shown in the diagrams below are the two blocks that we use to run the ends. Lateral blocking is shown in Diagram 55. Sweep blocking is shown in Diagram 56.

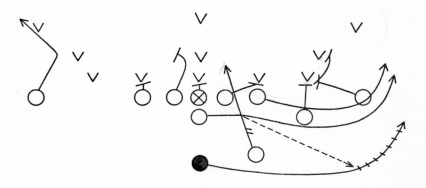

DIAGRAM 55.   Lateral Blocking.

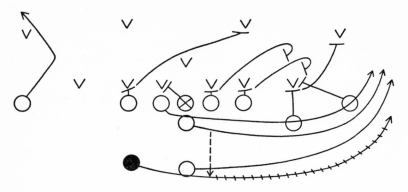

DIAGRAM 56.   Sweep Blocking.

WHY THREE BLOCKS IN EACH HOLE?

We use three different methods of blocking to open each hole because in this way we have been able to handle just about any type of defensive play we have faced. For example, when we are running our dive play, we will use man-blocking whenever possible. If the defensive man is too tough for our tackle to handle by himself, we will use quick-blocking.

When quick-blocking is employed, the guard will block from an advantageous inside-out angle on the tackle. The tackle will let our guard go first, then he will come up through the dive hole behind the guard's block. As he steps behind the guard, he immediately looks at the middle guard. If the center is having trouble with him, the tackle will fly into him and block him down the line, with the center as a post man. If the tackle sees that the center is having no trouble handling the man head-on him, he will go after the closest linebacker to the hole.

If this method of opening the dive hole is unsuccessful, we will attempt to use our trap block. When we use our trap block versus an odd defense, our center will post block for the guard, who executes the lead block. They can generally roll the middle guard successfully. To encourage the defensive tackle to come in, our offensive tackle in front of him will shoot inside through the line to block the nearest linebacker. The defensive tackle is allowed to come in free. Just as he thinks he is going to squash the ball-carrier, he is wiped out by the offside trapping guard. One of these blocks will usually prove effective.

Our tackles used to step around the defensive tackle to the outside, to influence him outside. Now our tackles will take a maximum split shoot inside, because shooting linebackers have caused us much trouble when they see the double-team block by the center and guard.

OPENING THE OFF-TACKLE HOLE

If we find it impossible to run plays to the inside of a defensive tackle, we will attempt to run our plays to his outside. Few tackles are exceptionally tough to both their inside and outside. They are usually instructed to protect either the inside hole or the outside hole, not both at once.

Using the same plan we used to run inside of the tackle, we will use our take-blocking at first. If our tackle cannot handle the defensive tackle by himself, we will use spike-blocking. Spike-blocking is a cross-block between our slotback and our tackle. This method of opening the hole places an outside-in angle block on the defensive tackle by our slotback. Our end will also execute this type of block when he is lined up in a tight formation.

If the tackle is too tough to handle this way, we will use power-blocking on him. The offensive tackle will stop the forward charge of the defensive tackle by coming up under his chest with both his forearms. He tries to stand the tackle up. The slotback comes into him with a full head of steam. Together they roll the tackle down the line and out of the hole.

There is always some weakness in every defense. As soon as our quarterback can find this weakness, he will go to work on it. With the different blocks available, the offense will find one that is most effective.

RUNNING THE ENDS

It was mentioned earlier that we use only two different blocking techniques for running the ends. The first one is called lateral blocking. Our onside tackle always pulls on lateral blocking; our guard fills for him, even if there is a man head-on our guard. If there is a man head-on our guard, our center fills for him. The entire offside of the line can slide one man down the line, if necessary.

The slotback will try to keep anyone in his area from crashing into the backfield. If the defensive end crashes into him, the slotback will hold him only until he sees the wide end coming down the line after him. He will release just a second before the wide end makes contact. The slotback will peel back on the outside linebacker. Sometimes the halfback will fake into the line, and other times he will lead the play. The offside guard will pull behind the line and attempt to get in front of the play. If he cannot get in front of the play, he will peel back on anyone filtering through the line pursuing the play.

The assignments for sweep blocking are slightly different. On sweep blocking we will pull both guards, unless there is a man head-on our onside guard, in which case he will stay in and block. The offside guard will pull on all sweep blocks. The tackle and the slotback to the onside will hold their blocks for two counts; then they will hurry to the onside flat and peel back on any pursuers.

When we face an even defense, each of these blocks is applicable. The linemen's rules will cover the slight changes in their assignments. Against an even defense we will use one additional type of blocking to hit up the center. This is shown in Diagram 57.

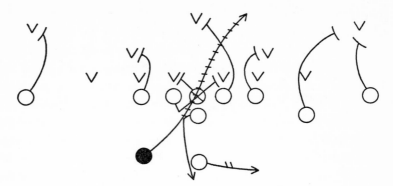

DIAGRAM 57.   Trap Blocking Versus an Even Defense.

WHO CALLS THE BLOCKS, AND HOW?

In the past we assigned the calling of our blocks to our tackles. This proved successful with some of the boys, but we could never teach block-calling to all of our tackles. Some of them who were adept at blocking and tackling could not think fast enough to do an adequate job of signal-calling.

Now, we have our quarterback call the blocks in the huddle. The rules that each lineman must learn help a great deal here. If a defensive man is not where he was, it makes no difference, since each lineman has a set of rules that will tell him whom he is to block, no matter what alignment the defense is in. Our attack has not suffered since our quarterback has been calling our blocking assignments in the huddle.

Our plays are called in the huddle in the following manner: The quarterback first calls the formation he wishes his backfield to get into. Then he calls out the series to which the play belongs; then he gives the play; then the blocking method to open the hole; and last he gives the snap signal. A play call will sound like this: "Flanker right, Red Series, 36, take, on 3."

This may sound complicated, but it is not. The quarterback will be able to call an intelligent game in a short time. It is better to spend a great amount of time teaching a couple of quarterbacks this material than it is to try to teach all the linemen when to use what.

The quarterback has three methods of opening each offensive hole. Any choice he makes should be adequate. Of course, one is usually better than others against certain defenses. Our tackles will be able to give him advice as to what type of block they can execute better, but this advice is only given when asked for. Some methods of blocking are better against an odd defense, and others are good against an even defense. If every man will learn his rules for opening each hole, the quarterback will seldom make a bad block call.

Our series helps the quarterback in his block selection. We will use one certain block on Red Series 36. We will use another block on White Series 26. When we run the ends, we generally use the same block.

The quarterback begins to associate certain blocks with certain series plays. For example, he will most always call Flanker Right, Red Series 36, Take-Blocking. If this does not work, he always has the other two methods to open the hole. This makes it much easier for all to learn; they associate the block with a series call. Wing Right, White Series 26, Power Blocking is another example of association learning. Flanker Right, Blue Series 28 Lateral Blocking is another play and type of blocking associated by our quarterback. If this block is not successful, he has others.

BLOCKING RULES

In our plan, we will be concerned with three positions of the defensive man, instead of four, as Coach Dodd's book, "Bobby Dodd on Football," suggests.

If we are planning to run a play off tackle, our offensive tackle will be concerned with three positions of the defensive man in his area: the man over him, the man in the gap to his inside, or the man off the line in front of him. This is shown by Diagram 57a.

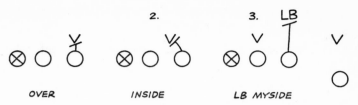

DIAGRAM 57a.   Play Off Tackle—Blocking Defensive Men in Three
Positions.

The diagrams illustrate that if a defensive man is lined up on
the outside shoulder of our offensive tackle, our tackle will never
be asked to block this wide man back to the inside. He may be
asked to block him out, but never back to the inside. If two men
are of equal ability, an offensive man will never get this type of
block accomplished.

The block that was shown in the previous diagrams was our
take-block. The tackle's rule for this block is over, inside, linebacker myside. This is what he does in the diagram. He blocks
a man over him; if there is no man lined up over him, he looks
to his inside. If there is no one head on him, or inside of him,
he will block the linebacker. These are the only defensive positions our tackle will be concerned with.

The defensive man who is on the outside shoulder of our
tackle will be assigned to an offensive man who is wider than
the defensive man—usually the slotback, but it may be the end
when he is in tight.

The slotback's rule on our take-block is illustrated in Diagram
58. The slotback's rule for our take block is identical to that
of the tackle; over, inside, linebacker myside.

It should be clear that in our rules a man is never asked to
block a player in who is outside of him. This man will be taken
care of by an offensive man who is wider than he is, or he will
be blocked from the inside-out by a pulling guard. This type of
block will allow us to run a play off the hip of our tackle or
slotback (see Diagram 59).

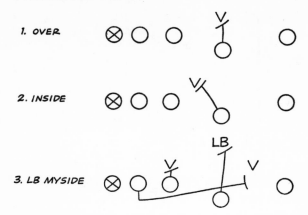

DIAGRAM 58.   Slotback's Rule on Take Block.

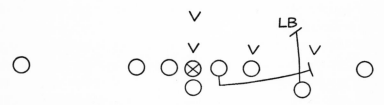

DIAGRAM 59.   Block from Inside-Out, on Man to Slotback's Outside.

BLOCKING RULES

Blocking Rule Terminology

The following terms must be memorized:

OVER:	Any man is over you if he is lined up head-to-head with you.
INSIDE:	Anyone lined up between you and your teammate closest to the ball.
OUTSIDE:	Any man who is on the line to your outside, but not past your teammate to your outside.
LINEBACKER MYSIDE:	The linebacker nearest the hole to my side of the line.
STRONG SIDE:	The side of the line to be attacked.
WEAK SIDE:	The side of the line away from which we plan to run.

PEEL-BACK BLOCK: A block executed by going deeper than
                          the defensive man you are assigned to
                          block, then blocking back toward the
                          line.

Blocking Rules for Centers

BLOCKS USED IN 1 AND 0, 2 AND 3 HOLES	ONSIDE RULE
Man Block	Over Strong side linebacker
Quick Block	Over Strong side linebacker
Trap Block	Over, post for guard Block to weak side

BLOCKS USED IN 6 AND 7 HOLES	
Take Block	Over Strongside halfback versus gap 8 fill to weak side
Spike Block	Over Strong side half versus gap 8 fill to weak side
Power Block	Over Fill to weak side

BLOCKS USED IN 8 AND 9 HOLES	
Lateral Block	Over Peel Versus gap 8 fill to strong side
Sweep Block	Over Fill to weak side

Blocking Rules for Guards

BLOCKS USED IN 1 AND 0, 2 AND 3 HOLES	ONSIDE RULE	OFFSIDE RULE
Man Block	Over Outside Middle L. B.	Middle L. B. Linebacker myside

Quick Block	Over Outside Middle L. B.	Middle L. B. Linebacker myside
Trap Block	Lead block for center Over Safety	Traps

BLOCKS USED IN 6 AND 7 HOLES

Take Block	Over Inside Linebacker myside	Strong side L. B.
Spike Block	Over Inside Middle L. B.	Strong side Half
Power Block	Over Inside Middle L. B.	Pull on end

BLOCKS USED IN 8 AND 9 HOLES

Lateral Block	Fill for tackle	Peel
Sweep Block	Over Inside Pull around end	Pull around end

Blocking Rules for the Tackles

BLOCKS USED IN 1 AND 0, 2 AND 3 HOLES	ONSIDE RULE	OFFSIDE RULE
Man Block	Over Outside Linebacker myside	Safety
Quick Block	Over if guard is covered Middle L. B. Outside	Safety
Trap Block	Outside linebacker	Check inside Peel

BLOCKS USED IN
6 AND 7 HOLES

Take Block	Over Inside L. B. myside	Safety
Spike Block	Cross block with end	Safety
Power Block	Post for end Inside gap	Bump inside Peel

BLOCKS USED IN
8 AND 9 HOLES

Lateral Block	Pull	Peel
Sweep Block	Hold two counts and pull	Peel

Blocking Rules for Slotbacks

BLOCKS USED IN 1 AND 0, 2 AND 3 HOLES	ONSIDE RULES	OFFSIDE RULES
Man Block	Align with hole and block out	Halfback
Quick Block	Align with hole and block out	Halfback
Trap Block	Middle L. B. unless no one is on tackle	Bump inside and peel

BLOCKS USED IN
6 AND 7 HOLES

Take Block	Over Inside Linebacker myside	Peel
Spike Block	Cross block with tackle	Peel
Power Block	Over Inside Lead block for tackle	Peel

BLOCKS USED IN
8 AND 9 HOLES

Lateral Block	Over, bump and peel	Peel
Sweep Block	Over, bump and peel	Peel

Blocking Rules for Wide Ends

BLOCKS USED IN 1 AND 0, 2 AND 3 HOLES	ONSIDE RULES	OFFSIDE RULES
Man Block	At halfback & out	At halfback & out
Quick Block	At halfback & out	At halfback & out
Trap Block	At halfback & out	At halfback & out

BLOCKS USED IN 6 AND 7 HOLES		
Take Block	Strong side half	Weak side half
Spike Block	Strong side half When spike is used away from slot-back, end is tight and cross-blocks with tackle	Weak side half
Power Block	Strong half, unless the play is going away from our slot-back. In this case, he will line up tight and help his tackles two-time block	

BLOCKS USED IN 8 AND 9 HOLES		
Lateral Block	Block back down the line and take first man to show wide	Down & out
Sweep Block	Block back down the line and take first man to show wide	Down & out

SUMMARY

With only eight blocks to learn and with such a simple method of teaching them as Mr. Dodd has devised, it is easy to learn all our blocking assignments. For many of the blocks the linemen will not even have three defensive positions to worry about. On trap blocking, for example, the trapping guard will do the same thing against all defenses. The tackle, when the lateral block is called, will do the same thing against all defenses. This makes their rules that much simpler to learn.

In the process of a game, we have very few missed assignments; hardly ever does a boy go for the wrong man.

CHAPTER SEVEN

The Quarterback

Quarterback is the most important position on any team. If this position is not filled by a capable lad, it will be difficult to field a successful team.

Some coaches feel that if the boy they have playing quarterback is incapable of calling signals, they will assign this important duty to some other position. There is nothing wrong with this; in fact, it may well be the only alternative. But if a quarterback isn't bright enough to call the correct play at the correct time, it is hard to imagine that he could be able to think through all the fakes he must execute.

The T-formation quarterback is in an ideal position from which to call signals. He is in the center of everything. From his central location, he is able to see the defensive alignment from an excellent vantage point.

Of course, this may not be the case if the quarterback is a pygmy playing behind a huge center or a monster of a middle guard. This situation actually occurred during one of our games. We had a small quarterback, a huge center, and the defensive middle man was a giant. Our attack up the middle was stopped cold. Our center and guards were not playing defense, so when we lost the ball and our defensive team took over, I called one guard over to me.

"Where, exactly, is that big boy playing?" I asked him.

"Head-on me," he said.

I informed him that the center had just told me that the big guy was playing head-on the center.

"That man is so big he is playing head-on both of us," he said.

STARTING A QUARTERBACK

We agree with Frank Leahy that the proper place to start teaching a quarterback his footwork and ball-handling is in the gymnasium. He gains confidence considerably faster by wearing basketball shoes on the smooth gym floor than by wearing football shoes with long cleats on a football field.

STANCE

To be effective, the quarterback must be comfortable in his stance. He must also be balanced. Comfort and balance are the first things on which we have our quarterback work. To be comfortable, he will stand as naturally as he can. We like our quarterback to stand as tall as possible. His feet will be about shoulder-width apart, or maybe a little less. The stagger of the feet is not too important as long as he is balanced.

The first few days, a center will not be necessary. The boys will work strictly on getting a well-balanced stance in which they can be reasonably comfortable. Any change will generally cause some discomfort. But this discomfort will soon be overcome by continuous repetition.

When the quarterback has a well-balanced stance from which he can be fairly comfortable, he will start working with the center. The center is brought in before the quarterback gets very far along, because if center and quarterback vary a great amount in size, the quarterback may have a slight adjustment to make with the center. It is my belief that if there is any adjusting to be done, the quarterback can do it more easily than the center. The center must also be a blocker, so he must assume a position from which he can also block. From this blocking position, he will deliver the ball.

The quarterback will stand as far away from the center as he can and still be comfortable. This is to keep some hard-charging defensive man from jarring the center back into him. From a step away, the quarterback can usually depart from the line before any defensive man can get to him.

Before the quarterback receives the ball from the center, he has mastered the following things:

1. He is well balanced.
2. He is as comfortable as possible.
3. He stands as tall as the center's size will allow.
4. He will be as far away from the center as he can comfortably be.

The quarterback is now ready to step in behind the center and get adjusted with him. If the center and the quarterback are of approximately the same size, no further adjustment will be necessary. If the center is a good bit shorter than the quarterback, the signal-caller will have to bend a little more at the knees to get in a good position from which to receive the ball.

HAND PLACEMENT AND STANCE

We have tried many methods of receiving the ball from the center. The method used at this time at Arizona State is this: The quarterback will reach forward with both arms, thumbs together. The heels of his hands are together; his fingers are extended and spread somewhat to form a pocket for the ball. The thumbs are placed in the center's crotch. The backs of his hands are pressing firmly against the top of the center's legs. Looking down, the quarterback should be able to see at least half his hand. If less than this is showing, he has his hands too far under the center's buttocks. If this happens, frequent fumbles occur, because the ball will be snapped past his hands.

When the quarterback has placed his hands in the desired position, his feet will be about a foot away from the center's. His knees will be slightly bent, his back straight, his shoulders square, his head and eyes up. He will have most of his weight up on the balls of his feet. The stagger is not too important, as mentioned earlier.

The only thing we insist upon concerning his footwork is that he learn everything he intends to do from whatever stance he does assume. To switch feet to execute different fakes can be fatal if a rival scout picks it up.

Quarterbacks have a tendency to form habits. It is a good idea to scout your own team to check on any habits your quarterback might be getting into. He may look at the hole he intends to attack. He may look in the direction he intends to run. He may wet his fingers when he is going to throw a pass. There are any number of things a quarterback may do that will give the defense the jump on the offense. If a team ever does pick up one of these give-away habits before we realize our mistake, they usually give us a terrible time.

When all these things have been learned, the quarterback is ready to receive the ball from the center. He has a few important reminders to help him. We call these reminders the three P's: Pressure, Push Off, and Pull Back—somewhat as Otto Graham describes in his book.

By pressure we mean the quarterback is to maintain constant up-pressure against the center's contact spot. If the pressure is felt, the center knows exactly where to place the ball. As the ball is centered, the quarterback will maintain this pressure. In other words, he will actually push the center off into his block as the ball is snapped. With this push-off action, the quarterback maintains contact with the center an extra second. This helps keep the quarterback from pulling away from the center before he has possession of the ball. When he obtains possession of the ball with his pressure and push-off action, he will pull the ball quickly back into his stomach.

These three P's—Pressure, Push Off and Pull Back—have helped cut our fumbles down by half.

THE BALL EXCHANGE

With the hands in the very natural position just described, it is necessary for the quarterback to receive the ball differently. The ball is delivered to him with the ends of the ball pointing up and down the field, instead of toward the sidelines. His hands are cupped with the heels together, the thumbs together, and the fingers cupped and spread slightly. This method of receiving the ball actually closes the fingers around the ball as it is snapped into this pocket.

Chapter 5 on Interior Line Play contains more information concerning this type of ball exchange.

MOVING AWAY FROM THE LINE

Getting the ball from the center is the easiest thing the quarterback has to do. Now that he has the ball, his real work begins. To be able to move away from the line as quickly as possible is naturally the goal. We have our quarterbacks drill on pushing off with the forward foot if the staggered stance is used. If the toe-to-toe stance is used, the push-off is with the offside foot. Our best results have been achieved by having the quarterback take his rear foot clearly off the ground and push off hard with the forward foot. As the push-off is made, the rear foot goes in the intended direction. This is really just a leap backward. It stresses the push-off with the forward foot. This type of push-off drill helps develop quickness in executing both the front and the reverse pivot.

We use the front hand-off and the reverse hand-off. When the front hand-off is used going to our right, the push-off foot is the left foot. When we use the reverse pivot hand-off going to our right, the push-off foot is the same. The importance of this drill is that it gets either front or reverse pivot under way much quicker.

On either one of these hand-offs, the quarterback will turn his head quickly as far around as possible in the direction of the back who will receive the ball. This gives him an instant longer to see the spot where he will deliver the ball and enables him to place the ball in the correct position. This extra split-second saves hurried, fumbled hand-offs. The quarterback will turn his entire body in the direction of the approaching back before he even moves his feet. This shows how quick the move is.

We use both front and reverse pivots on all our plays. The reason why we use both is that many times a middle guard will have a tendency to move with the quarterback's first step. If the middle guard is doing this, a reverse pivot will get him going in the desired direction, and the center or one of the guards will have a much easier time blocking him.

All of our series of plays can be run from these two simple take-off methods. With just a simple additional step or two, all the fakes necessary for any of our plays can be executed from these two pivots.

Every coach has his own ideas about footwork, so it will not be necessary to go into great detail on this phase. Diagrams 60-69 show the three main series we run and illustrate the types of pivot is used.

Both the front and reverse pivots are employed when the Red Series is used.

For all Red Series plays, the steps are the same through the first fake. When the fake has been made to the halfback as in play 22, all that is required to get the ball to the fullback on play 36 is one additional step with each foot.

When play 38 is used, the first steps are also identical to those required for play 22. When the fake has been made to the halfback, the quarterback immediately pitches the ball out to the fullback who is on his way around the end.

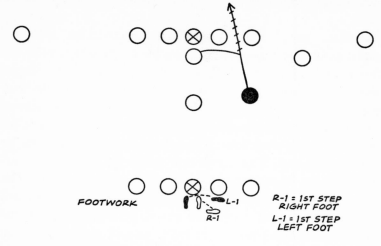

DIAGRAM 60. Play 22 Front Pivot (Red Series).

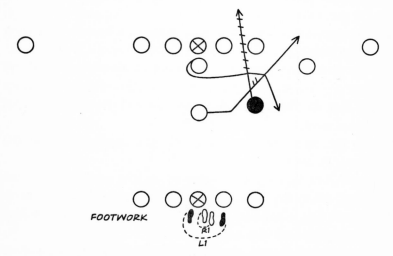

DIAGRAM 61. Play 22 with a Reverse Pivot (Red Series).

The footwork for the fullback cutback play is shown in Diagram 62.

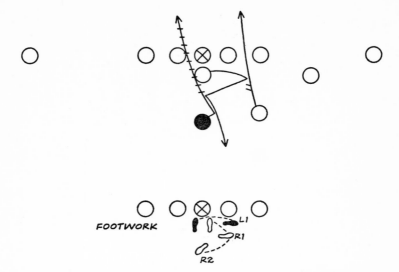

DIAGRAM 62. Play 31 Cutback Front Pivot (Red Series).

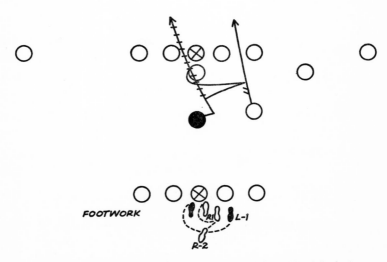

DIAGRAM 63. Play 31 Cutback Reverse Pivot (Red Series).

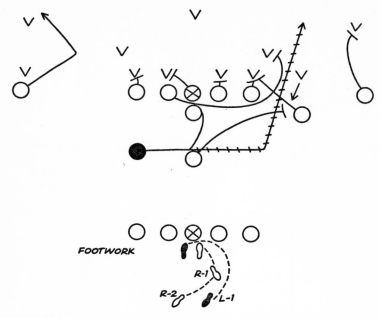

DIAGRAM 64.   Play 26 Front Pivot Only (White Series).

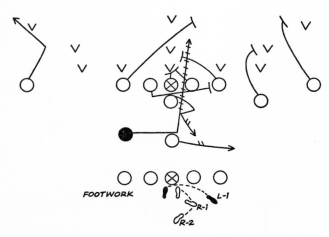

DIAGRAM 65.   20 Trap—Front Pivot (White Series).

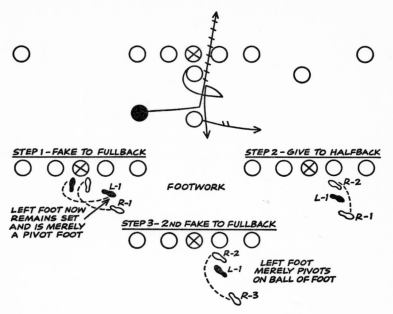

DIAGRAM 66.   20 Trap—Reverse Pivot (White Series).

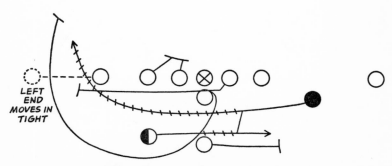

DIAGRAM 67.   Play 247 Front Pivot Only (White Series).

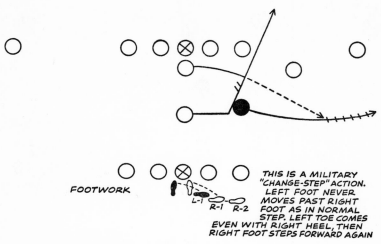

THIS IS A MILITARY
"CHANGE-STEP" ACTION.
LEFT FOOT NEVER
MOVES PAST RIGHT
FOOT AS IN NORMAL
STEP. LEFT TOE COMES
EVEN WITH RIGHT HEEL, THEN
RIGHT FOOT STEPS FORWARD AGAIN

DIAGRAM 68.   Play 28 Front Pivot (Blue Series).

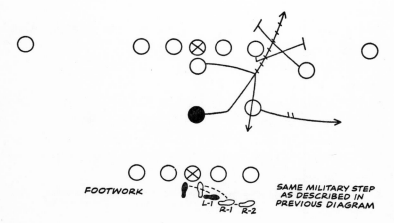

SAME MILITARY STEP
AS DESCRIBED IN
PREVIOUS DIAGRAM

DIAGRAM 68a.   Play 36 Front Pivot (Blue Series).

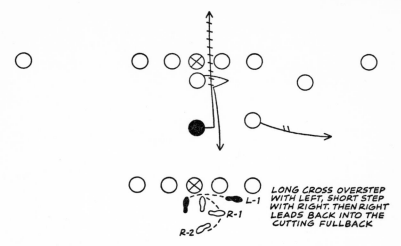

DIAGRAM 69.   30 Trap—Front Pivot (Blue Series).

SUMMARY

To summarize the important factors needed in a quarterback:

1. He must be intelligent.

2. He must have a real love for the game and be willing to devote many hours of hard work, physical and mental.

3. His stance must be comfortable and adjustable to that of the center.

4. His voice should be strong and clear. His attitude should command respect.

5. He should stand as far away as comfortably possible from his center.

6. He should never change his feet for different maneuvers.

7. He should master the three P's—*pressure* to the center's buttocks; *push off* with center's move forward; and *pull back* of the ball from the forward position he has it in, when he gets the final exchange.

8. He must learn, by practice, quick foot movement away from the line of scrimmage.

CHAPTER EIGHT

Quarterbacking
the Slot T Offense

As our quarterback masters his offense, the team becomes more difficult to defend against. There are countless possibilities in each of the different offensive formations. The quarterback can pick the defense to pieces after he learns enough about the Slot T offense.

In high school, two or three series of plays are adequate. A dozen plays in all should suffice.

If the quarterback will study the adjustments the linebackers make to his slotback, he can make his battle plans. If defensive players overshift their strength toward the slotback, we have several key things to find out. Are they overshifting to the flanker, regardless of the position of the other backs? Do they rotate their deep backs to a flankered slotback? Do they always make the same type of adjustment to the slotback? As soon as the quarterback or the scout in the press box can determine this, we have a few things on which to base our plans.

It takes many hours of hard work by the coach and the quarterback. There is no short-cut to teaching the quarterback what he must know to make this offense really productive. If the quarterback knows the offensive possibilities of each of our backfield formations, the defensive alignments become less and less worrisome.

Our quarterbacks are taught one series of plays on the blackboard, and they are not allowed to go on to another series until they know this phase letter-perfect and know the alignments it will work against. They always start with Red Series, which consists of five plays. Most of these five plays can be run from almost all our offensive formations. This series is shown from each of our main offensive formations in Diagrams 70-85.

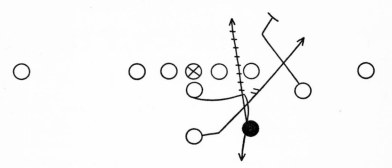

DIAGRAM 70.   Play 22 Flanker Right (Red Series).

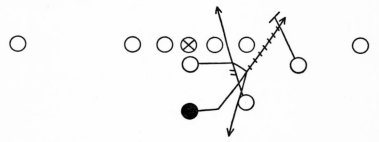

DIAGRAM 71.   Play 36 Flanker Right (Red Series).

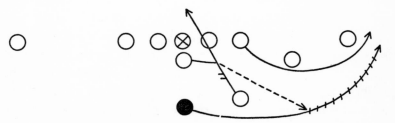

DIAGRAM 72.   Play 38 Flanker Right (Red Series).

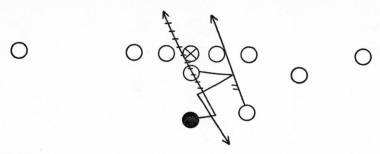

DIAGRAM 73. Play 31 Cutback from Flanker Right (Red Series).

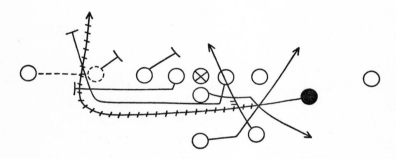

DIAGRAM 74. Play 47 Flanker Right (Red Series).

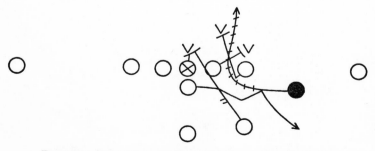

DIAGRAM 75. Play 42 Flanker Right (Red Series).

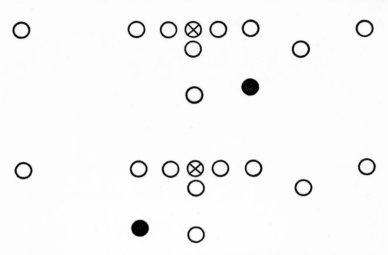

DIAGRAM 76.   Red Series From Wing Right Formation.

With the movement of one single offensive man, as shown in Diagram 76, the defense is faced with an entirely different picture. This is the strength of this free-wheeling offense.

The defense is now forced to adjust their alignment. They do not like to do this; most teams prefer to stay in one defense. If they are forced to adjust continually, they are not as sure of themselves as they will be if they are allowed to stay in one defense. The plays that can be run from this formation are shown in Diagrams 77-81.

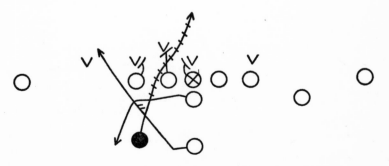

DIAGRAM 77.   Play 23 Wing Right (Red Series).

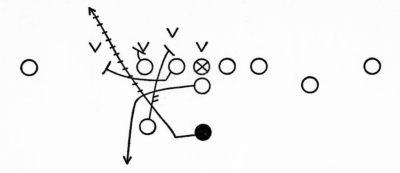

DIAGRAM 78. Play 37 Wing Right (Red Series).

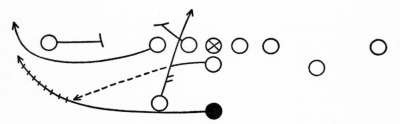

DIAGRAM 79. Play 39 Wing Right (Red Series).

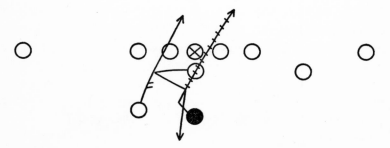

DIAGRAM 80. Play 30 Cutback Wing Right (Red Series).

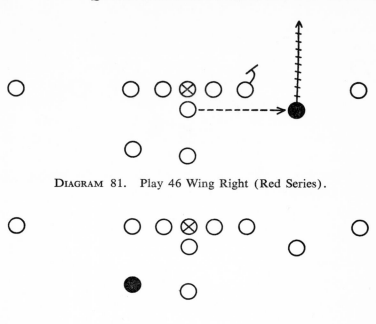

DIAGRAM 81.   Play 46 Wing Right (Red Series).

DIAGRAM 82.   Red Series From Wing Right Split Formation.

Again, with the movement of a single man on the offensive team, we have given the defense a new problem. Now, as can be seen in Diagram 82, the offense has a dive back on each side to contend with. This forces the linebackers to respect the straight-ahead power. If they must stay and protect the dive hole, the possibility of passing behind them and running around them is a little better.

Some of the Red Series plays that can be run from this split formation are shown in Diagrams 83-85.

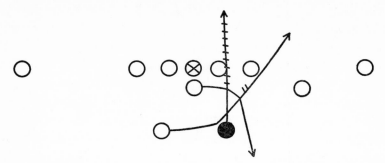

DIAGRAM 83.   Play 22 From Wing Right Split (Red Series).

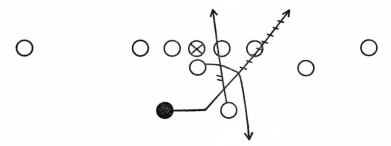

DIAGRAM 84.   Play 36 From Wing Right Split (Red Series).

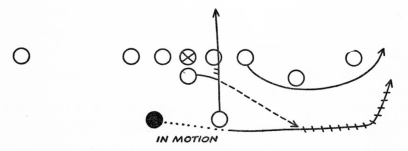

DIAGRAM 85.   Play 38 Wing Right Split (Red Series).

When the quarterback has mastered the Red Series and knows each play that can be run from it, he is ready to move on. The confidence that is shown by the quarterback after he knows the one series thoroughly will astound you.

A good test of how well he knows this series is this: Draw a defense for one of the formations on the board. Have him pick out the weak spots and call the plays he would use against this particular defense. This is an enjoyable and profitable exercise. He will say, "Against that defense I would run such-and-such." Or he might say, "That defense is dead versus this play." The quarterback will look forward to these meetings.

When we feel that he knows the Red Series perfectly, we move on to the White Series and repeat the operation, then on to the Blue Series.

AUTOMATICS

Our method of getting a play under way at the line is helpful in teaching our quarterback to think. He is constantly on the lookout for a better play selection than the one he called in the huddle. This has been valuable in teaching our boys to be flexible and use their heads.

The passes that are quickly available add to the excitement of trying to find a weak spot. The wide ends are in such an advantageous position to receive passes that they are constantly a threat. The quarterback always keeps his eyes open and knows if the defense covers the ends. A defensive slip here, and the quarterback can engineer an easy touchdown. Pressure is always maintained on the defense.

We have a simple and effective method of calling our automatics. If a play has been called in the huddle and, after arriving at the line of scrimmage, the quarterback finds the call impractical or sees a better opportunity, he will change it.

How? In the following manner: To get our team placed in a down position at the line, the quarterback always shouts out two double digit numbers and a color. The two numbers may or may not give the team a message. The color is always the signal to get down from the hands-on-knees position to the blocking position, and it may also give the name of the new series to be run.

The quarterback will always shout out these two numbers, and the team will always completely disregard them—unless the first of the two numbers is the number of the play that was called in the huddle. If play 22 was called in the huddle, and if he sees that this was not a good call, all he needs to do to cancel it is to call 22 first when he is at the line. If any other number is called first, the huddle play will be run.

How do we call a new play when the play is canceled? If the first number called is the same as the huddle play, this cancels the huddle play, and the second number called by the quarterback is the new play. The color called next is the series from which the new play will be run.

Let us take an example: If play 22 Red is called and the play is not practical, it is necessary for the quarterback to call 22 as his first number at the line. This immediately alerts the team that play 22 is canceled, and they intently listen for the second number called out. This second number is the new play. Now they listen to the color called out by the quarterback, which tells them from which series the new play is to be run.

When play 22 Red is called in the huddle and the quarterback at the line shouts "22—36—Blue," 22 cancels the play, 36 is the new play, and Blue tells the backs that their fakes will be the Blue Series fakes.

This automatic system is excellent training for the quarterback. He will look over the defense in search of something better than his huddle call after he gets the team to the line. If he sees a better possibility than the play called in the huddle, he can change it easily. The system of automatics will soon tell a coach whether or not his quarterback understands the offense.

SUMMARY

To use the Slot T to its fullest advantage, the quarterback must be able to move his offensive personnel around to take advantage of defensive adjustments to his slotback. If they adjust too much, he has certain things to do; if they fail to adjust enough, he has other things to do.

If the defense fails to cover the wide ends closely, they are in excellent position to score on one play. The quarterback can always stay ahead of the defense because he knows the weaknesses of most of the defenses his team will face.

Quick passes to the wide ends on look-in patterns will force the outside linebackers to be conscious of this pass. This, in turn, will make the running plays more effective. A linebacker cannot cover well on passes and be thinking strong rushing defense at the same time.

Our quarterbacks can present the defense with a different problem by simply moving one man. This shifts its strength and, if the defense ignores this shift, the offense can move the ball effectively over the weakened spot. If the defense does move a man to cover the new threat they may be in an unfamiliar alignment, and they will not be a strong unit.

The automatics give the quarterback an easy and simple system of using new weaknesses he has found in the defense. When he finds a weakness, he will decide which play he wishes to run and call it out at the line of scrimmage.

CHAPTER NINE

The Slot T Rushing Attack

It is important, when planning any offense, to have some variation. The offense must be flexible enough to be able to exploit any defensive weakness; it must include enough variety to keep the defense guessing. The defense should never be allowed to get set and dig in.

We have been able to keep opponents loose by using four to six different backfield and flanker formations. These formations are simple to learn, and they do not require a single change in the line. The formations we use force the defense to readjust continually. Even though they may have to move only one or two men, it gives us an advantage to worry them, even by forcing a minor readjustment. The more formations the defense is forced to prepare for, the less time they will be able to spend concentrating on one defense.

Diagram 86 illustrates what we call our "flanker right" formation.

The quarterback can align his team in this formation by calling "Flanker Right" in the huddle. His call in the huddle will

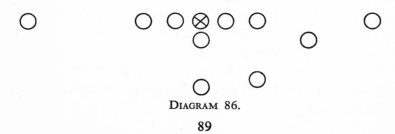

DIAGRAM 86.

89

sound something like this: "Flanker Right, 22, Red Series, man blocking, on two." This command tells the team members the formation they are to assume at the line, who will carry the ball, through which hole he will carry it, the type of blocking to use, the fakes the other backfield members will execute, and the count on which the ball will be snapped.

On flanker right formation, the ends are spread about ten yards. On occasion, the end away from the slotback will line up only about two yards from his tackle, or "in tight." The slotback will take his position one yard off the line of scrimmage and facing the defensive tackle, as explained in Chapter Thirty. His distance away from the offensive tackle will vary constantly; we do not want him to line up in the same position for any length of time. His constantly changing position will become of great concern to the defense before long, and this helps us.

Our halfback will place himself in the dive position behind our right tackle. He is three and a half yards from the line of scrimmage.

Our fullback's position is behind the quarterback, approximately four yards from the line.

The flanker right formation is our bread-and-butter formation. To defend against it, the opposition must overshift its defense and move an extra man over to the side of our flanker.

Diagrams 87 and 88 show our end-run play against an overshifted defense and a balanced defense.

There is a method by which it can be determined fairly well whether or not the defense is overshifted. Draw an offensive alignment on the blackboard, and place any defense against it that you feel is practical. Then draw a perpendicular line through the fullback, quarterback, center, and on through the defense, so the line extends beyond the deepest defensive back. Then count the men and see which team has the most men on either side of the line. If the defense has the most men on either side of the line, that is an overshifted defense. Diagrams 89 and 90 demonstrate this point.

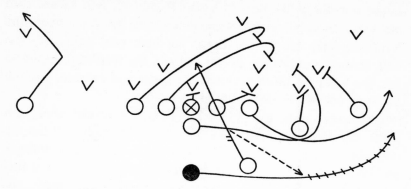

DIAGRAM 87. Flanker Right Play 38 Versus Overshifted Five.

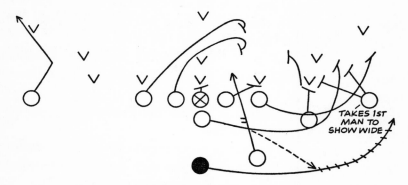

DIAGRAM 88. Flanker Right Play 38 Versus a Balanced Five.

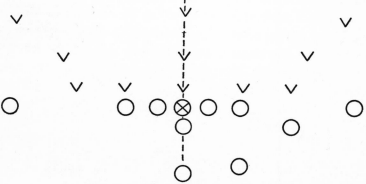

DIAGRAM 89. A Balanced Defense.

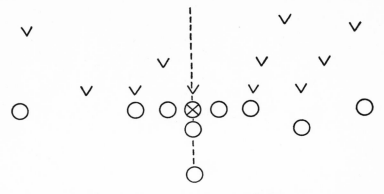

DIAGRAM 90.   An Overshifted Defense.

From our flanker right formation, we have been able to run the off-tackle hole quite consistently. Diagrams 91 and 92 show this off-tackle play, first against a balanced five-man front, then against an overshifted five-man front.

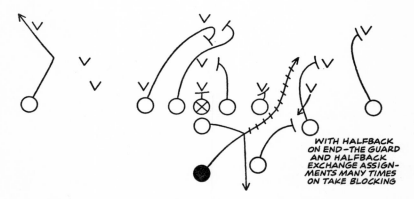

WITH HALFBACK
ON END–THE GUARD
AND HALFBACK
EXCHANGE ASSIGN-
MENTS MANY TIMES
ON TAKE BLOCKING

DIAGRAM 91.   Flanker Right Play 36 Versus Balanced Five.

The dive play is an effective play against most defensive alignments. The blocking for this play is almost identical against a balanced defense or against an overshifted defense. For this reason, Diagram 93 shows only the blocking against an overshifted defense.

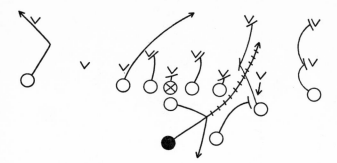

DIAGRAM 92. Flanker Right Play 36 Versus Overshifted Five.

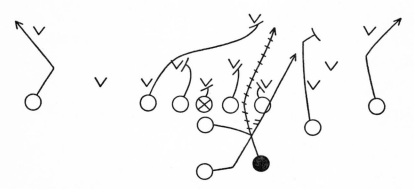

DIAGRAM 93. Play 22 Versus an Overshifted Five.

From the diagrams of the plays shown, it is evident that the defense must overshift in some way to stop the three plays just diagrammed. What can be done if the defense does overshift? What if they stop the three bread-and-butter plays? What can be done to take advantage of this overshifted defense?

We attempt to exploit the overshifted defense in two or three ways. One way is to use a reverse, which runs effectively against an overshifted defense (see Diagram 94).

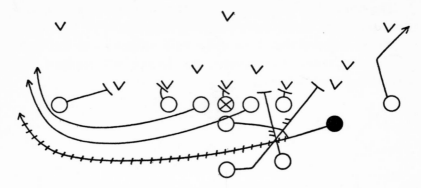

DIAGRAM 94.   Flanker Right Play 49 Versus Five-Man Line.

Another play we use to exploit the weakness of an overshifted defense is the quarterback option, away from the flanker. This play is shown in Diagram 95.

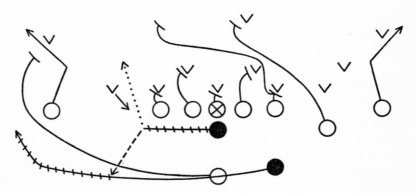

DIAGRAM 95.   Flanker Right Play 17 Option Left Versus Overshifted
Five.

If the defense has shifted so much with the flanker that our wide left end is covered by only one deep man, we can hurt them with a pass. An end who is talented to any degree can get free for a pass against a one-on-one situation. He will, in this case, take an exceptionally wide split to give himself considerably more room in which to maneuver.

The third plan we use to attack the overshifted defense is a flood pass back to the weak side (see Diagram 96).

We have found that if we come back effectively to the weak side several times in succession, the defense will readjust into something more balanced.

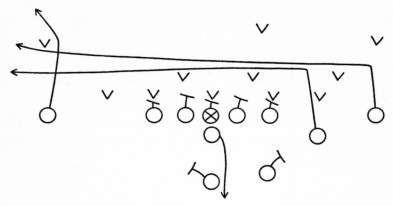

DIAGRAM 96. Flanker Right Flood Pass to Weak Side Versus Overshifted Five.

The first three plays shown here—the end run, the off-tackle, and the dive—are all plays from the Red Series. This is the series we use to find the weak positions on defense. If we can make our Red Series work, we will not bother to use anything else. Of course, each play that has been diagrammed has a duplicate play to the other side. Anything that can be run to the right from flanker right can be run to the left from flanker left formation.

If the defense always adjusts to the flanker the same way, regardless of the position of the remaining backfield members, we like to run our plays from a slightly different backfield set-up. We call this our Wing Right Formation.

Diagram 97 clearly shows that the wing right formation is much better balanced than is the flanker right formation. The same plays that were diagrammed earlier using our flanker right

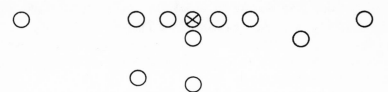

DIAGRAM 97. Wing Right Formation.

formation can also be run from wing right formation. Against some types of defenses, the wide end will have to be lined up in a tight formation. These plays are shown in Diagrams 98-100 from a wing right formation. From wing left, of course, the same plays may be run to the opposite side of the line.

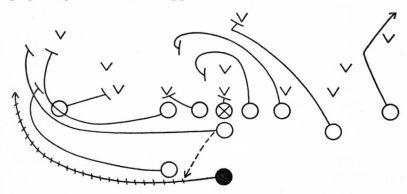

DIAGRAM 98. Wing Right Play 39 Versus Five-Man Line.

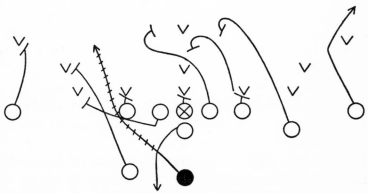

DIAGRAM 99. Wing Right Play 37 Versus Five-Man Line.

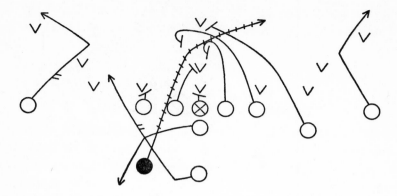

DIAGRAM 100. Wing Right Play 23 Versus Five-Man Line.

Our power series of plays, the White Series, are run from this wing formation. This formation is so well balanced that it forces the defense to balance up also. If they fail to balance up, we can exploit this failure; the offense can do more from the wing formation than from the flanker formation.

Diagrams 101-104 show some of the plays from White Series that we have been successful with.

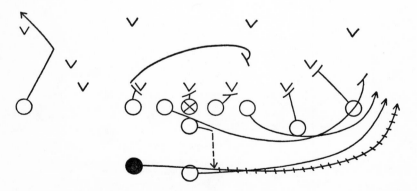

DIAGRAM 101. Wing Right Play 28 White Series Versus Five-Man Line.

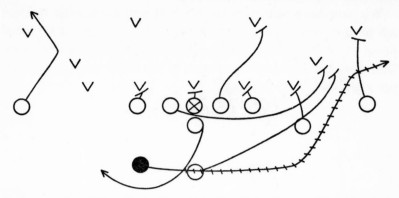

DIAGRAM 102.   Wing Right Play 26 White Series Versus Five-Man Line.

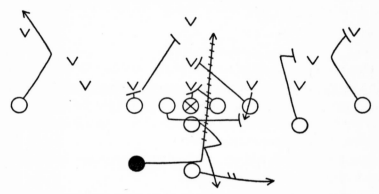

DIAGRAM 103.   Wing Right Play 20 Trap White Series Versus Five-Man
Line.

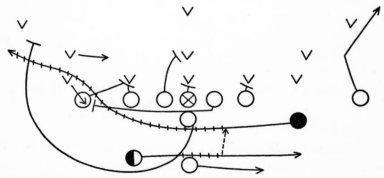

DIAGRAM 104.   Wing Right Play 247 White Series Versus Five-Man Line.

We have been able to move the ball well from wing right or left formation, using the above plays and including a few special passes to help keep the defense a little more position-conscious. Diagrams 105 and 106 show some of the better passes from this particular offensive alignment.

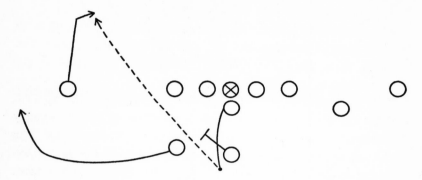

DIAGRAM 105.   Wing Right Pass—Quick Post to Left End.

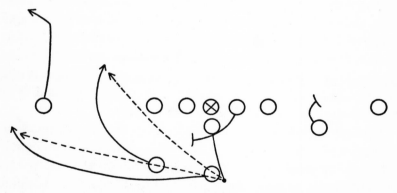

DIAGRAM 106.   Wing Right Pass—Quick Corner 2 Back Curl
3 Back Swing

These two passes illustrate how easy it is to move the ball by passing if the defense makes the wrong move.

The third formation from which we run a few plays is called

the Split Formation. This formation involves only a slight change by one man in our backfield. When the split formation is called, the fullback will move over to the vacant dive position. This presents a slightly different problem for the defense, for there is now a dive back behind each tackle. This will force the defense to place their linebackers a little differently than on either our flanker formation or our wing formation.

This formation is more like the conventional T formation, in that we have two dive backs. In both the flanker and wing formations, there is only one quick-hitting back available; in the split formation, there are two.

This formation is very effective for the passing game as well. Almost any pass than can be run from either of the previously mentioned formations can be run from the split formation. The backs are in excellent position to swing to either flat or to curl up in the center. They are also in fine position from which to meet a defensive end on pass protection.

The fourth formation that is employed by our quarterback during the progress of a game is called the Double Wing Formation. This formation is easy to assume at the line of scrimmage. There is only one adjustment: The halfback away from the slotback will move out and up to within a yard of the line of scrimmage. He will vary his width from his own tackle, as does the regular slotback. His assignments on running plays and pass patterns are the same as those of the slotback.

Almost any play that is used with any of the other formations is easily incorporated into this one. This is done by running the halfback in motion toward his regular slotback. The timing can be worked out to place the halfback in just about any position desired. Diagram 107 shows how a wing right play can easily be run from a double wing formation.

In Chapter Ten, the passes that can be used from our double wing formation are discussed, so they will not be explained here. Shown below in Diagrams 108-110 are some of the running plays that can be run from the double wing formation.

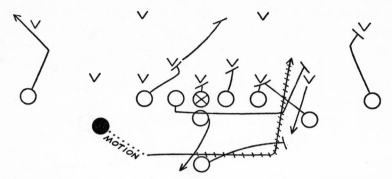

DIAGRAM 107. Double Wing 26 White Series Versus Five-Man Line.

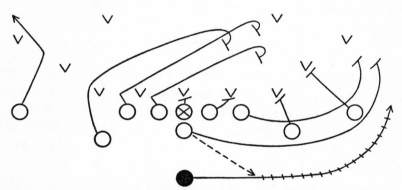

DIAGRAM 108. Double Wing Play 38 Red Series Versus Five-Man Line.

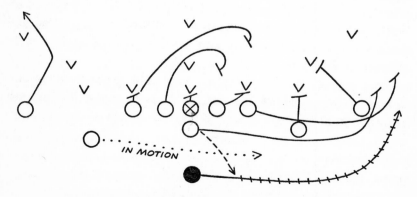

DIAGRAM 109. Same Play with a Halfback in Motion.

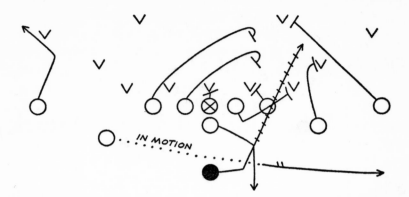

DIAGRAM 110.   Double Wing Play 36 Versus Five-Man Line.

SUMMARY

We have tried to show how we can take advantage of just about any type of defense by moving our offensive backs around to advantageous positions. If the defense fails to adjust properly, our quarterbacks are taught what should be done to exploit the resulting weakness. This takes many painful hours of hard work with our quarterbacks, but we feel that it pays dividends.

We will not delve into what can be done against specific defenses. Each coach has his own ideas on what play will work at what time against what defense. The thing we have attempted to show here is this: By moving our men around, we cause the defense a great deal more work and worry to defend against each offensive formation.

Each formation places a certain amount of pressure on certain defensive personnel. If the defense fails to make the proper adjustment, our quarterbacks can take advantage of their failure.

CHAPTER TEN

The Slot T Passing Attack

In the previous chapter, most of the time was spent trying to deploy the offensive personnel in such a way as to make the rushing game more difficult to stop. Perhaps as you perused the chapter, you thought of defensive strategies that would halt such rushing maneuvers. This happens on the football field as well—but against the Slot T offense, it can be dangerous for the opponents to overstress any single phase of their defense. If they are overzealous in trying to stop the rushing game, this type of offensive deployment offers far more versatility in exploiting their defensive strategy.

The ends are advantageously positioned to get behind a defensive backfield that is too intent on coming up recklessly to make tackles. They are also in good position to block back down the line. A good block by a wide end can wipe out two or three would-be pursuers.

The slotback is in good position to spring into the open. From his position, one and one-half yards off the line of scrimmage, it is difficult for a defensive man to keep him from moving into a pass pattern; he has more room in which to maneuver and free himself from a defender assigned to keep him on the line of scrimmage. One or two good fakes and he can even swing past the finest linebackers.

All that is necessary to break a defense out of its tight alignment is to complete one or two long-gaining passes to one of the wide-spread ends or to the slotback. The slotback is in almost as good position as the wide ends.

If the rushing defense places so much pressure on the passer that he cannot throw from his pocket behind the line, it is possible to have our quarterback roll out and throw on the run. This roll-out maneuver gives him more time and allows the receivers more time to fake and try to get into the open. If the defense rushes too hard, it is susceptible to screen passes and quick pitchouts around the end, with great come-back blocking possibilities from the wide-spread end to the running side.

It is our opinion that from the Slot T, a team has more additional weapons than does any tight formation. A defensive plan cannot be set up effectively if more stress is placed on defense against passing than against rushing, or vice versa. With the proper personnel for the Slot T, the balance of the defense becomes more necessary. It is my opinion that we can run more effectively against a balanced defense from our Slot T than we could from a Tight T, and we have proven to our own satisfaction that we can pass more effectively from the Slot T than we can from a Tight T.

The defense can be forced into balance more easily from the Slot T than from the Tight T. Against the Slot T, it is much more difficult for the defensive personnel to hold offensive players on the line of scrimmage, and thus to allow the deep backs to come up closer. If the potential pass-receivers can be held up effectively, the deep backs can naturally come up closer to the line of scrimmage, where they can be more effective against running plays in addition to covering receivers until the line gets the passer.

Place the three eligible pass-receivers in a position where they are difficult to contain, and the deep backs must respect the scoring potential. Any of the three receivers can catch a pass for a touchdown if the defensive halfbacks get too zealous in their attempts to stop the rushing game. This is what balances the defense.

If the defensive backs line up too tight, we can pass effectively. If they hang back too deeply, we can run. If they balance up, we can do both more effectively from the Slot T than we can from the Tight T. Why? Because the Slot T spreads the defense and allows our pass-receivers more room in which to maneuver, and it also has the personnel in key positions, in a compact group, to unleash an effective rushing attack.

We do not feel that our players at Arizona State are supermen. What we are trying to emphasize is that we do not believe we could have been able to get to the Holiday Bowl in St. Petersburg, Florida, using any other offense. We believe that a good team using another formation can be a better team using the Slot T.

The player who convinced us that the pass could and should be used more than on third down was a youngster named Layton Ducote, now making a name for himself in professional baseball. He could throw a football so accurately that he transformed a dull, listless group of high school players into an exciting, alert, hard-hitting team that won four straight ball games after he started at quarterback for the first time in midseason.

It was so easy to move the ball by passing that a revolutionary revision of our offensive thinking started. We were running from our spread out of desperation, because we could not make any other type of offense move the ball. But with this fine quarterback, and passing from the spread, the aerial game really became an integral part of football for us.

In 1955, I had the privilege of working with one of the finest passers in the Southwest, John Ford. We were both serving as assistants to Warren Woodson at the University of Arizona. John Ford had set all kinds of passing records while playing for Mr. Woodson at Hardin-Simmons University, and he was helpful in convincing me that the easiest method of advancing the ball in football was by the forward pass.

Many teams plan their passing attack around a fake running play. They feel that to be effective in throwing the ball, they first have to make the defense think in terms of stopping a run.

This is good logic, but it can be overdone. When it is an obvious passing down, it is practically useless to fake a running play; it is more effective to get the pass on its way. What *can* help is to spread the offense even farther than usual. This forces the defense to spread and, even though they know that the play is a pass as soon as the quarterback gets the ball, the extra spread makes the job of defending against it that much more difficult.

PATTERN SELECTION

We have always had a difficult time trying to get our quarterbacks to select the proper receiver on a pass pattern. It seemed that more often than not he was caught with the ball while trying to decide which choice was better.

We have set patterns for our pass-receivers to run. Sometimes three men are sent out, sometimes four, and sometimes two. And sometimes we will send out only one receiver. On any pass in which two or more receivers are involved, we name the pass. Our "60 pass," for example, is one of our plays with three men in the pattern. They will each have a certain pattern to run. Usually one of the men will be most likely to get into the open more easily than the others. This man becomes the number one target. The number two target will be the receiver who is next most likely to be free, and so on.

This pattern type of pass-calling helps the quarterback to watch for the most likely receiver. After the defense adjusts and stops our pet pass plays, the quarterback has a simple way to make a new pass pattern with one single change. He will simply say, "60 pass, left end hook and in the hole." The other receivers run the normal pattern they run on all 60 passes.

PATTERN PASSES

We have had reasonable success with only four or five pass patterns. If the quarterback is able to change any one of the pass receiver's patterns to meet emergencies, it is readily seen that from these few simple patterns at least three times that number of plays can be run. When the pass play is called in the huddle, each receiver will run his predetermined pattern unless the quarterback gives him another pattern to run. This is so the men who are not primary targets will not run a pattern that could get them into the path of the intended receiver.

Diagrams 111-116 show a few basic pass patterns that have worked well for us.

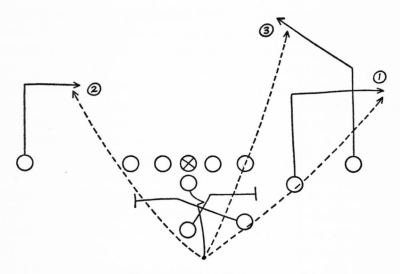

DIAGRAM 111. 60 Pass.

PATTERNS ALL RECEIVERS ARE TO KNOW

Shown in Diagram 112 are the maneuvers that each potential pass-receiver must know. These are known to our players as our single calls, and they may be executed by any given player. They are usually used in conjunction with a pattern type of pass. They are effective when a pass defender is susceptible to a particular type of maneuver by an offensive pass receiver.

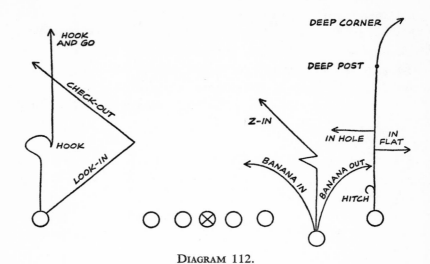

DIAGRAM 112.

DIAGRAM 113.   61 Pass.

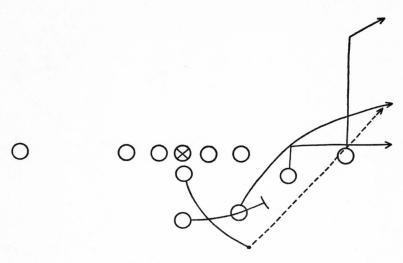

DIAGRAM 114.   62 Pass.

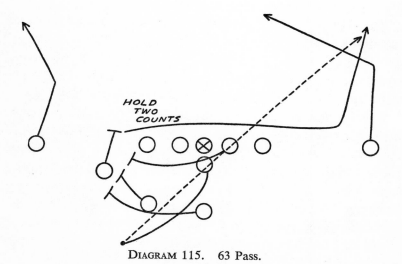

DIAGRAM 115.   63 Pass.

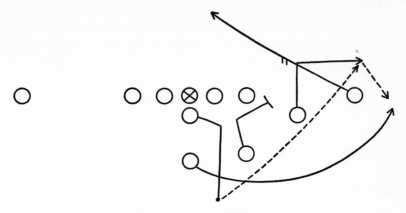

DIAGRAM 116.   64 Pass.

WHO CALLS THE PASSES?

For the most part, our quarterback calls the passes. It has been suggested that the ends can call a better pass than the quarterback, since they know when and on what pattern they can get open. We allow this to a degree, but we do not condone actual play-calling by anyone other than the quarterback.

The ends are merely allowed to suggest the maneuver which they think will free them best from the defenders. An end might tell the quarterback, for example, "I can get free on a Z-in pattern when you need it." Such information is vital, and the quarterback certainly appreciates suggestions of this nature.

This freedom on the part of the pass-receivers to make suggestions helps in getting them to work hard on their faking when they are not the primary target. It has a tendency to encourage each of them to see what maneuver he can work on the defensive back in front of him. He will experiment on him to see whether he can get free on a down-and-out pass, or whether a hook-and-go will fool him. He may try to run straight at the defensive back to see how fast he backs up; this might tell the end that he can get behind his man, or it might tell him that the hook pass is a cinch, because the back is too deep-pass conscious; and so forth.

These suggestions by the ends are never made in the huddle. No word is ever spoken in the huddle by anyone other than the signal caller. All suggestions are made to the quarterback before he comes near the huddle.

PASSING DRILLS

The following passing and pass-receiving drills have been of help to us.

Umbrella Drill

On this drill, five receivers are placed in front of the quarterback, approximately where the open spots are in an umbrella defense. The defensive men will take their normal positions between the offensive men in the four-deep secondary, as shown in Diagram 117.

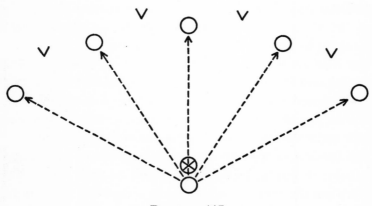

DIAGRAM 117.

The quarterback will fake to one or two of the men in front of him and try to draw the defenders away from one certain receiver. As soon as the ball is in the air, it is free, and all the defenders try to get to the ball before the receiver has it. This gives the defense great experience in really hustling toward the ball after it leaves the quarterback's hand. It is also a valuable drill to teach the receivers to catch the ball under great pressure. This turns out to be a real battle: The ends work hard to conquer "hearing footsteps," and the defense is determined to keep the receivers from catching the ball.

Much helpful information comes from teaching the passdefender just how much ground it is possible to cover after the ball is in the air. All that is necessary to benefit from this particular phase of the game is to back the passer away from the receivers ten or fifteen yards. We have found, believe it or not, that a defender can cover at least half the distance the ball travels on a normally-arched pass. Knowing this, they try harder to knock it down.

Pass Interception Drills

Diagram 118 shows a drill that will do more to help the defenders realize their capabilities in getting to a ball that is in the air than any I know of.

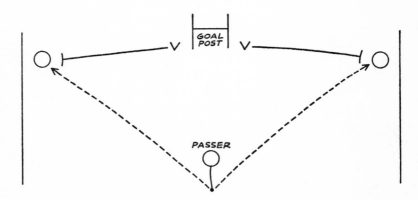

DIAGRAM 118.   Pass Interruption Drill.

The receivers are located in the coffin corners of one end of the field. The pass-defenders are standing by their goal posts. The passer stands back approximately fifteen yards to start with. He shoots a pass to either receiver. The defender nearest the receiver darts for the corner, trying to arrive in time to knock the ball down or intercept it. If he can get to it, move the quarterback up a step and repeat. If he cannot get to it, drop the quarterback back a step.

This gets to be a real contest between the pass-defenders. They are proud of how much territory they can cover. It is also a good drill to teach receivers to catch the ball under pressure, for the defensive backs really come barreling after them.

Most quarterbacks come out early for practice and get all pass-receivers in two lines and throw to them. Much good can be accomplished in this type of drill (see Diagram 119). Receivers can work on the points where they are weak. Some will work on their faking, others on catching the ball properly, and others on getting away from the line faster.

A quarterback who will really work can improve himself 100 percent by hustling back to the pocket each time. Many boys have a tendency to get lazy doing this and form bad habits.

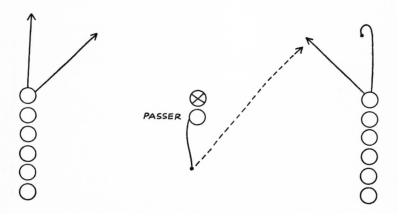

DIAGRAM 119. Two Line Drill.

It is a good idea to time the quarterback to keep him conscious of this most important phase of the game. He should be timed when he fakes to crossing backs, and also when he just drops straight back. Three seconds will usually be enough time to get the pass off.

We use three different plans from which to pass. The first, shown in Diagram 120, is the straight dropback.

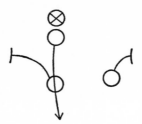

DIAGRAM 120.   Straight Dropback.

This is the type of pass protection we try to give the passer when it is an obvious passing down—third down and fifteen, or more. When we use this pass-protection blocking, we spread our ends and slotback to the maximum. This allows them more room in which to execute their fakes. We will generally try to run one of our wide receivers on a spot pattern. The quarterback will try to look away from the intended pass-catcher with a good fake, as if he will actually throw the ball to the offside receivers. He will then turn and throw the ball to a designated spot on the field. The receiver may not even be close to this spot when the ball is thrown; he will be making his fakes and setting up the defensive man for his quick cut into the path of the ball. Diagrams 121 and 122 show two passes of this type.

PROTECTION FROM A RUN FAKE

In the second plan, we try to make the defense think the play coming at them is a run, as long as we possibly can. This keeps the defensemen from putting on a real concentrated rush, since they have territories to protect against running plays. It also has

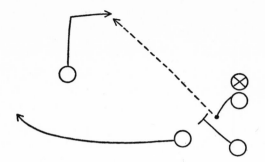

DIAGRAM 121.   Quick Post.

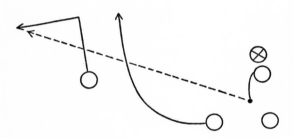

DIAGRAM 122.   Left End Square Out.

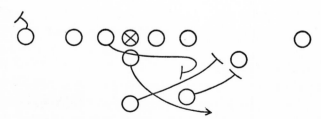

DIAGRAM 123.   Roll-Out Pass Protection.

a strong tendency to make the defensive secondary move up closer to help stop the run. Occasionally, if the fake run is well executed, a pass-receiver will be down the field all by himself. Many teams have a pass from each running play they use.

Diagram 123 shows our roll-out passing formation. This has been our bread-and-butter passing formation, for the simple reason by which we were forced into using it: Our passers have been so short it has been difficult for them to see from a pocket behind the line. We rolled them out as shown above, so they could see their intended targets better. Flood passes, where we try to place more receivers into a zone than there are defenders, have been more successful from the roll-out, which has also proved a more effective way to pass against a strong rushing defense.

EXPLOITING THE DEFENSE FROM VARIOUS FORMATIONS

It was mentioned in Chapter Nine that the defense must be careful how it overshifts to flankers. We use four to six separate backfield alignments, each designed to force the defense into just a little change on the part of one or more defenders. If the defense fails to adjust, we can exploit this development; if the defense does adjust, we can usually exploit some new weakness.

Our quarterbacks are taught the strengths and weaknesses of our offensive system. We attempt to teach them what we think is a sound defense against our system of offense. We know what we can do best, and if the defense does not come up with a plan to stop what we can do best, we feel that we can generally win.

In Chapter Nine, we listed the formations from which we run the ball. In Diagrams 124-135 are shown a few of the passes we use to keep the defense honest.

Pass Plays to Exploit a Strong Overshifted
Defense Against Our Flanker Right Formation

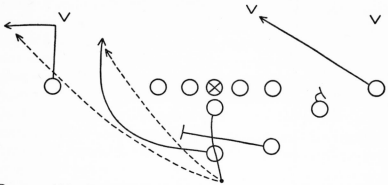

DIAGRAM 124.   Pass to Left End Sideline Fullback Curl Flanker Right.

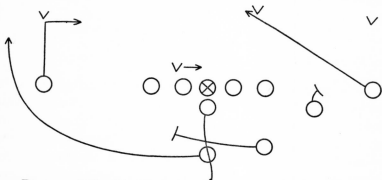

DIAGRAM 125.   Flanker Right Pass Left End in Hole Versus
Overshifted Defense.

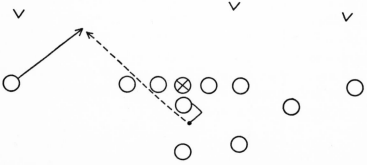

DIAGRAM 126.   Pass—Look-in to Left End Versus Overshifted Defense.

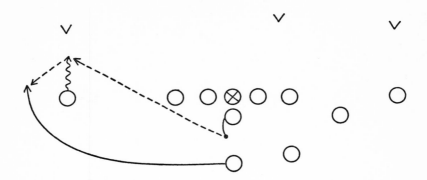

DIAGRAM 127.   Pass—Hitch to Left End Versus Overshifted Defense.

Pass Plays to Exploit a Defense That Does Not Adjust
Properly to Our Wing Right Formation

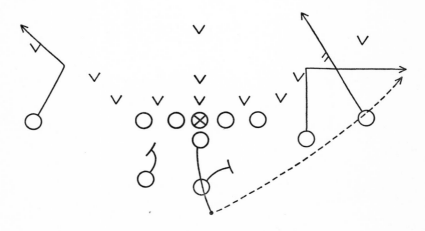

DIAGRAM 128.   Pass 66.

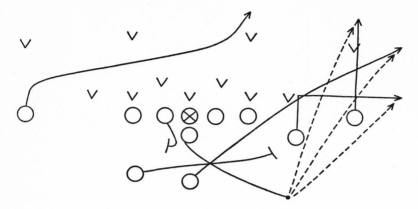

DIAGRAM 129.   Pass 62 Versus 5-2-4.

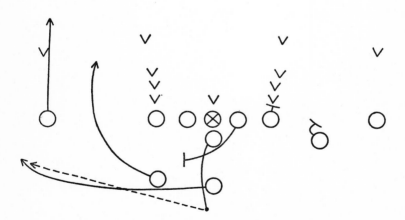

DIAGRAM 130.   Pass 67 Versus Stunting Defense.

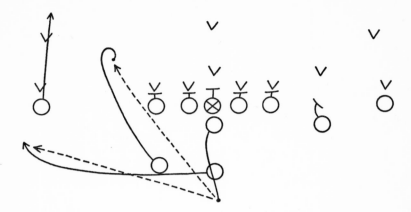

DIAGRAM 131.   Pass 68 Versus 6-2-3.

Passes That Can Be Used Effectively
from the Double Wing Formation

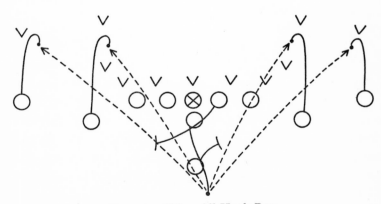

DIAGRAM 132.   All Hook Pass.

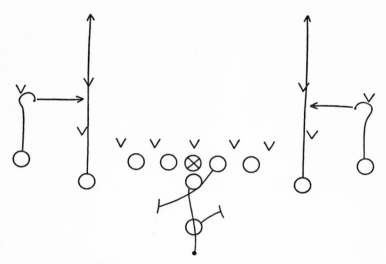

DIAGRAM 133.   Outside Hook and In Hole.

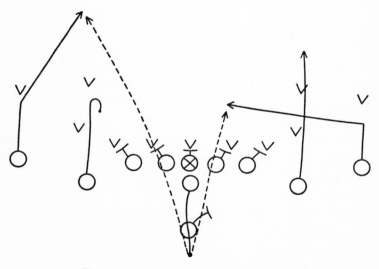

DIAGRAM 134.   Pass Double Wing 69.

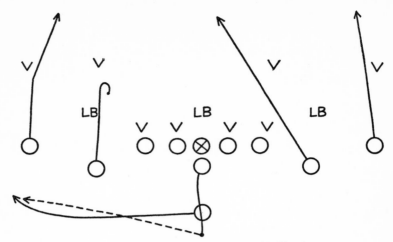

DIAGRAM 135.   Swing Pass to Fullback.

These diagrams indicate some of the passing possibilities of this type of offense. Being able to place pass-receivers into the open so quickly against unrealistic defenses is the real strength of this offense.

SUMMARY

The Slot T gives us the necessary tools to pass against any type of defense that is also sound against a rushing offense—and if the defense gets too determined to stop our passing, we can switch to a powerful rushing game, as well.

We have proven to our own satisfaction that we can do everything from this formation as well or better than we could from a Tight T formation.

The different offensive backfield alignments make the defense vulnerable; that is, the defensemen must contend with quick-striking passes to one of the several available pass-receivers, and they must also be alert for a quick dive by one of the backs. This type of offense thus forces better balance on the part of the defense, and this makes the defenders easier to pass against and, at the same time, easier to rush against.

CHAPTER ELEVEN

Kicking from the Slot T

The kicking game is an exciting phase of football. It can be even more exciting from the Slot T, because it can be utilized more frequently (if need be) and more safely from this spread-type offense than it can from others.

Many coaches overlook the importance of their kicking game. It can be a definite asset to a team with a good kicker. At one time, I must confess, I did not recognize the true importance of kicking. But circumstances (which is another word for experience) changed my mind. I have seen a talented quick-kicker keep us in such hot water that we barely escaped with our hides. We would be on the verge of getting out of trouble when boom! —a quick kick would put us back in the hole.

However, punting and punt coverage have been lifesavers for us, too. We have had more than our share of success with the spread punt formation.

Since we have free (NAIA) substitution in most of our games, it is possible for us to get our fastest men into the game when we punt.

Diagram 136 shows our spread punt formation. By having our fastest backs on the line, we have been able to get wonderful punt coverage and very little average return. In fact, not one punt was returned for a single yard during the entire regular season in 1958. This was because we had a fine punter, Ted Sorich, who averaged something like 35 yards per kick. He

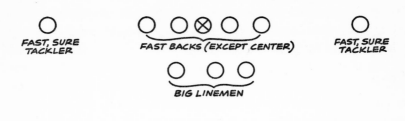

DIAGRAM 136.   Our Spread Punt Formation.

would boot the ball so high that it almost brought rainfall—
and when the ball came down, there were usually seven of our
players waiting to get the receiver. That was the trick that helped
us tremendously in our undefeated season.

SPREAD PUNT ASSIGNMENTS

Center

The center, of course, snaps the ball. Usually he will rock
forward to get enough leverage to snap the ball deep. If he does
this in rhythm, the defense can prime itself on the forward rock
and charge with the ball. To nullify this defensive advantage and
still give the center the help of the rock, we have him rock forward, then hesitate as he sees fit before snapping the ball. When
the kicker is ready, he will give him a hand signal, and the center
will snap the ball any time after he gets the signal.

The Guards

The "guards," who usually will be two of our fastest backs,
will split as far as the first man to the outside of the center will
split with them. The first man outside the center is the player the
guards are assigned to crack. They will bump their man just long
enough and hard enough to get him off balance.

A count of "one thousand and one" is sufficiently long for the guards to maintain contact with the opponent. As soon as they have made this contact, they will sprint for the punt receiver. They will try to force the receiver to choose a direction—to go in one direction or the other so the other members of the team will be able to come in under a full head of steam. If the receiver is quickly forced to move in a certain direction, the pursuit of the other linemen can be more vigorous, and the trap closes swiftly and surely.

This attempted forcing of the receiver is an outright gamble on the part of our guards. They must not let the receiver pick his own return pattern. If the receiver has a blocker or two in front of him to protect the catch, it is the responsibility of the guards to blast into them at full speed and try to bounce them back into the receiver.

Two of the most accomplished "blasting" specialists I have ever seen, Mel Huffaker and Ray Harris, normally two linebackers, could put the pressure on punt receivers exceptionally well. They would use an offensive shoulder block to boom the protectors. Their initiative and aggressiveness could thwart any hopes for a punt return by the ball-carrier.

The Tackles

Here, again, we place some of our fastest men. The tackles will spread away from their own guard as far as the second defensive man outside the center will permit. If the defender will spread with them, they can move out three or four yards. If this is impossible, the tackles must be in a position to hold their opposites for the same "one thousand and one" count before releasing and streaking downfield as fast as possible. They will maintain their respective positions as they roar after the receiver, who will have been forced to choose a path due to action of the guards.

The tackles should be on the scene just in time to put the stopper on the receiver as he attempts to avoid the guards.

Usually, if the punt is down the middle, the tackles will be on hand a split second after the guards have blasted through. The receiver may be undecided as to which way to start his return. If the punt is as high as we want them all to be, there will seldom be a return of any consequence.

The Ends

This is an important position on any punt coverage. If the end gets careless and commits himself too quickly to the inside, we are in serious trouble. The end must never converge on the runner until he has seen that the ball-carrier cannot possibly get around him.

The ends may spread as wide as they wish before the snap. If the interior linemen will slow their opponents, the outside defenders cannot get into the backfield quick enough to block the punt.

The end's responsibility is to make certain that no one gets around him with the ball. This must be emphasized and re-emphasized, for all ends have an inclination to go after the receiver in a big hurry.

The real secret to this spread type of coverage is not to boot the ball too far. Believe it or not, we have had better luck covering the 35-yard kicks than we have the 55-yarders. If the punt is too long, the receiving team can form their return before we can cover.

The Three Deep Tackles

These three fellows line up about five yards behind the line of scrimmage. They will separate just far enough to allow the ball to get past them so the punter can catch it. As the ball is snapped and goes past the tackles, they pinch together. Each tackle hits the first man to show in his respective area. All three must be careful not to back up, or else they may get kicked in the seat of the pants by the punter.

The tackles are able to take the jar of the onrushing opponents better than the backs. The smaller backs, on the line of scrimmage, are close enough to the opposing (and larger) linemen so that their inertia has not had a chance to become a factor. Consequently, our backs are seldom injured on these punt-formation plays.

TIGHT PUNT FORMATION

For obvious reasons, we use the tight punt formation when we are forced to kick from inside our five-yard line. The tight punt is shown in Diagram 137.

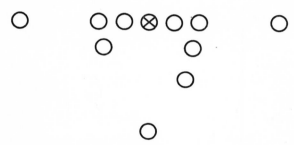

DIAGRAM 137.   Tight Punt Formation.

The tight punt formation is the safest only if the punter cannot get his full 14-yard depth from center. If he can get the desired distance, it is my opinion that he can boot the ball just as consistently from the spread as he can from the tight formation.

However, when this depth is impossible or when the end zone line is too close for comfort, we will kick from the tight formation.

Center

The center's responsibilities are the same as for the spread punt. He will snap the ball when ready, but only after the punter has indicated that he is ready. When we punt from a tight formation, it is generally because we are in trouble.

We always snap the ball on a long count or a long delay. If a scheme to block the punt is in the offing by the defense, this may force them to show their hand and give us an opportunity to see where the pressure is going to be placed.

The Guards

The guards in a tight formation will be our regular guards. They will line up shoe-to-shoe with the center. When the ball is snapped, they will block to the inside. They will not block individually; that is, they are not responsible for any certain man. They are responsible for the area to their inside. They must not allow any defensive man to get between the center and themselves.

The Tackles

The tackles will be the regular tackles when we punt from this tight formation. They will line up shoe-to-shoe with the guards and be responsible for their inside. They must not let anyone come between them and their guard to the inside. They are responsible for positions, not people.

The Ends

The ends will spread the same as they do on spread formation, unless the halfback defending to his side calls for an end to come back tight and help protect the area to his side. If the defense loads up on the short side—the side away from which our two backs are lined up—our end to that side must come in tight and force the defense to rush around him.

The end on the side of the two backs will always be free, and he is the "forcer." He will disregard the wide responsibility that is his on the spread and will shoot directly for the spot where the ball is being caught if our kicker fails to get it out of bounds. He will blast through the man protecting the receiver, the same as our guards do from our spread punt. The one wide end cannot let himself be knocked down by the linebacker or the halfback; if he is the least bit talented, this should never happen.

The Backs

The backs will be deployed in this way on our tight formation: Our halfback will place himself just to the inside of our left tackle; he will take the first man to show outside of the tackle. Our slotback will place himself just to the inside of our right tackle; he will take the first man to show outside of the right tackle. The fullback will place himself just to the inside of and about three yards deeper than the slotback. He will place himself in a position where he can receive the ball on a direct snap from center, if needed. This presents the possibility of the fullback carrying the ball and surprising the opposition. The fullback will block the first man to the outside of his slotback on the punt play.

The backs will fan to the deep outer areas of the field as soon as the ball is kicked and will assume the end's responsibilities. They will never allow any ball-carriers to their outside.

The linemen will hold for counts of "one thousand and one, one thousand and two" (two counts), then will release and fly to the receiver, always maintaining their respective positions on the field.

Real scrap and hustle is the secret of adequate punt coverage from a tight formation. We would rather see the punter boot the ball out of bounds if possible. It is not often that a punter of this calibre can be found. In 1960, we had an excellent punter— Mike Mercer—who could boot the ball almost any place he wanted, but such punters are rare.

NCAA SPREAD PUNT

The spread punt we use, when we are playing under NCAA rules with limited substitution, is the same as that we utilize with free substitution, with the exception that we are unable to immediately replace everyone with faster men. So we keep our men in their normal positions. When we are unable to take advantage of fresh players on punting situations, we would rather have our guards blasting through the receiver protection than face the possibility of our running backs getting hurt. Diagram 138 shows the system we use when playing under NCAA rules.

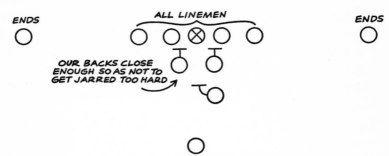

DIAGRAM 138.   NCAA Spread Punt.

Notice that the three deep men are in a different position than they are when we punt from a spread under free-substitution rules. The backs are now the three deep men. We station them closer to the line than we would our larger linemen—because we do not want the defense to get a good start—then slam hard into them. This coverage has proven quite successful, but not quite as good as the free substitution type, where faster men can be utilized.

SLOT T QUICK KICK

For many years, I was not particularly interested in the quick kick. I felt it would be an admission that we couldn't move the ball—that yielding the ball one down early meant taking away a chance for a possible touchdown play. It meant that right away we were on defense, and I disliked the thought of defense. I wanted that ball; you can't score without it.

Well, that was a few years ago, and I have learned to appreciate defense. We can score from defense too, I learned. Two years ago we had a fine defensive backfield—Al Alvarez, Rudy Calrere, Louis Casillas, and Bill Herrera—who called themselves the "Chihuahua Backfield" because all four were of Mexican lineage. In ten games, they intercepted 26 passes. Al Alvarez intercepted 12 himself. When you multiply these twenty-six passes by four, you get 104 potential offensive plays they took away from the offense. That could be 104 potential touchdown plays. Subtract this amount from the ten game total, and it becomes evident that defense is really important: An average of ten and four tenths plays per game were taken away from the offense—and any one of these plays could have beaten us.

With this in mind, we don't mind giving up the ball to our opponent when forced to punt.

Our spread Slot T affords an excellent formation from which to employ the quick kick. The ends are already spread and in position to cover the quick kick immediately. The fullback does the quick kicking when we boot from any of the formations shown in Diagrams 139-141.

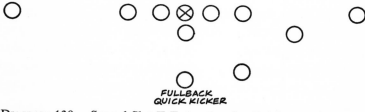

FULLBACK
QUICK KICKER

DIAGRAM 139.   Spread Slot T Formation for Quick Kick (Fullback Quick Kicker).

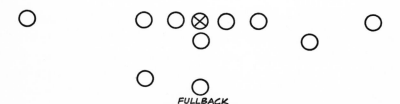

FULLBACK
QUICK KICKER

DIAGRAM 140.   Fullback Quick Kicker.

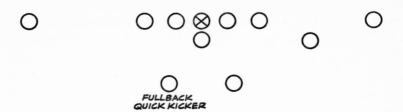

DIAGRAM 141.   Fullback Quick Kicker.

The quarterback does the quick kicking when we are using formation shown in Diagram 142.

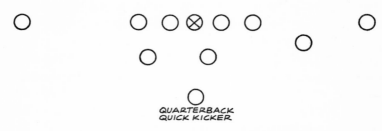

DIAGRAM 142.   Quarterback Quick Kicker.

As can be seen, the latter two formations are also wonderful to pass from. This means that the defense must play it honest; they will not dare "cheat" and send a man back in anticipation of a quick kick, because this also is a forward-pass situation. If the safety man gets too anxious to cover what he believes will be a quick kick, the quarterback can fake the quick kick and hit an end in front of the deep safety. Deploying men in this fashion keeps the return to a minimum when we do punt. It also gives us three or more men downfield quickly to recover a fumble or take advantage of a bobble.

QUICK KICKING

Our quick kickers usually boot with more distance from their rocker-step motion than they do when they are deep and have all the time they need. A few years ago I had a junior college transfer from Texas who quick-kicked a bit differently than I had ever seen it done previously. As he received the ball from the center, he turned and faced the defensive end. He placed the ball at a right angle to his foot and kicked with his instep on the "white stripe" area. This gave the ball an end-over-end movement, and he got exceptional roll out of his kicks.

We have had more consistently long rolls from our regular quick kicks, however. The principal difference is that the kicker, from his standing position, takes a rocker step backward with his left foot. Then he rocks forward with the same foot and booms the ball with his right foot. With this quick action, he does not move much closer to the line of scrimmage than where he stood originally. He meets the ball the same as he does in a regular punting situation and tries to spiral it, hoping to get the tail down as it hits ground to accelerate the roll in the proper direction.

QUICK-KICK PROTECTION

We have our linemen block aggressively and low when we intend to use the quick kick. This action keeps the defensive linemen from penetrating into the backfield and has a tendency to make them keep their hands down to fight our blockers.

The halfback to the side of the foot with which our punter kicks will make certain that no one rushes the booter from his side. He will then sprint downfield to cover the kick. This is true for the slotback, also, if the backs are deployed over a spread area with only the fullback in the backfield.

When the quarterback is under the center, he will spread his legs wide enough to allow the ball to pass through. He will then move away from the leg that the kicker intends to use. This will prevent him from accidentally deflecting the ball, and it will also serve as a distracting move to fool the opposition and prevent a determined rush after the kicker (see Diagram 143).

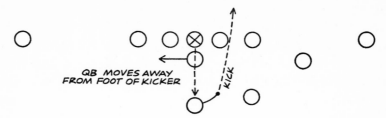

DIAGRAM 143.   Distracting Move by Quarterback on Quick Kick.

SUMMARY

From the Slot T offense, it is possible to have a much better coverage for our kicking game from the spread punt formation.

This is a formation from which we can always threaten a quick kick. The fast coverage from the Slot T is really worthwhile. If the defense starts playing for the quick kick when it is third down and we have long yardage to go by dropping a man back to receive it, we are still very dangerous with a forward pass to any one of our widespread receivers. They make it almost impossible for the defense to drop a man back, thus making the quick kick more effective.

CHAPTER TWELVE

Preparing for the Season

Getting off on the right foot for the long, hard football season is one of the most important assignments a coach can have. There are many minor items that need attention. If a coach is not careful, he may forget some of the most important tasks.

HOW AND WHERE DO WE START?

All players will be invited to be on campus the day before football season starts. It is important to have everything ready for them when they arrive. Boys who are away from home for the first time are always lonesome and blue. If things do not go smoothly at this early period, you can lose some of your finest prospects.

We do not believe in pampering our ballplayers, but we would like to have a good look at them before they depart for home. If they are allowed to leave our campus with ill feeling, it may hurt us in their community in the future if we want to talk to another prospect. If they do leave our campus, we hope it is because they are not capable of making our team. If this is the case, they will usually not hold any hard feelings.

When players first arrive on our campus, we have someone meet them and show them to their rooms. After they have settled themselves, they will be taken to the cafeteria. This is the place they all love. We try to keep them busy the first few days to keep their minds off home and the sweetheart they left behind.

One of the most vital meetings is conducted the evening before our first practice. Here, they become acquainted with our offense. This is an appropriate time to emphasize what is expected of them on and off the field. We have found that if football players know what is expected of them, they will usually behave quite well.

Our first meeting will be our get-acquainted meeting. We will have our veterans stand individually, for introduction to the new freshmen. The freshmen have generally read a great deal about these veterans. When they get the chance to meet them, their first impression is that they are a part of the team.

We point out what it takes to be a Lumberjack. We stress how much sacrifice it takes, how many, many candidates have tried and have failed. We emphasize that not just anyone can be a Lumberjack. This information has a great bearing on the type of attitude the new boys will start practice with.

As soon as these items have been covered, we get into the meat of the meeting. Each boy gets a special notebook for his position—six or seven notebooks go to the quarterbacks, centers, and fullbacks, and approximately twice this number for the tackles, guards, ends, and halfbacks.

Each notebook contains a page of rules for the particular position and some history of our school and our football background. We want each candidate to feel that it is a great privilege to be a Lumberjack. On this page is also explained what we think should be the prospective athlete's attitude toward Arizona State College and the faculty. We have had wonderful cooperation from the faculty. Therefore, we will not tolerate any player who is not also willing to cooperate 100 percent.

The remainder of the book is filled with pages of blank play diagrams, as shown in Diagram 144.

As we start our play explanation on the blackboard, the players copy each play in their notebooks. They will be held

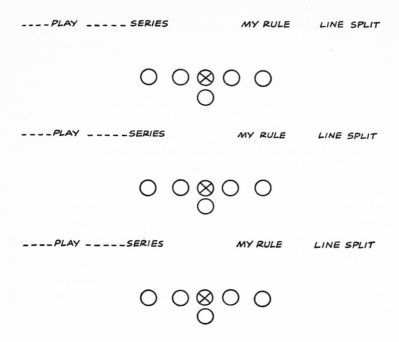

DIAGRAM 144. Blank Play Diagrams.

responsible for knowing their assignments letter-perfect. The first week, the new boys are required to carry their notebooks with them wherever they go. They are quizzed at any time and at any place. If they fail to know any of their assignments, they get a lap around the field for every mistake they make. This is incentive enough to encourage them to know their assignments. Most football players do not relish running "punishment" laps.

The first night provides a good opportunity to take the new boys to the stadium so they can be outfitted with uniforms. This will save time, and time is of great importance during the first two or three weeks of practice. It seems we never have enough time; we will not waste a precious second if we can avoid it.

We try to get everything taken care of the day before practice starts, so that we can go right into the meat of football in the very first practice. We do not want to waste half a day waiting for the players to get suited out.

In the past, we have held Press Day or Picture Day the day before practice started. This also saves valuable time. Our press man has been so cooperative in the last year or so, however, that we have been able to sandwich pictures in between other activities. These people often annoy a busy coach, but it is necessary for them to get the pictures they need if we are to have the proper type of publicity. They, like the coaches, have a job to do. (See Chapter Fourteen on the Coach and the Press.)

THE FIRST DAY OF PRACTICE

With all the preliminaries out of the way, we can now bear down on the drills we explained the previous night. We want the players to have these theories come to life before them on the field.

On the blackboard the night before, we covered probably no more than three plays. Going slowly like this makes it possible for the players to absorb the plays more readily.

Many coaches spend a great amount of time in the early fall stressing calisthenics. It was my experience while a player that if these calisthenics were of long duration, they took so much out of me, I had little to finish practice on. Since I started coaching, I have made it a policy to have no organized calisthenics before practice. Before the season starts, we write each boy and give him a few simple exercises that we feel are valuable. We suggest that he come to camp ready for football. We explain we will not have time to condition him after he gets here, and we want him in shape and ready to go when he gets here.

Our practices will start with the boys loosening up on their own. When practice starts, we expect them to be loosened up and stretched and ready to go. This saves a lot of time. We will usually start by running the boys around the goal posts a couple of times to make sure they are loose. We have them pull their knees up extremely high. As they run, they will get plenty of arm and shoulder action to insure a complete warmup. This helps eliminate pulled muscles.

GROUP WORK

For the first few weeks, the coaches are on the field for nearly ten hours a day. With only one assistant coach to help, it has proven valuable to conduct practice in three groups.

We divide the players into groups. The backs practice for one and one-half hours—usually from 8:30 to 10:00 A.M. The line will also practice for one and one-half hours each morning —usually from 10:00 to 11:30 A.M. The ends practice for one hour, from 11:30 to 12:30.

Lunch will be served from 1:00 to 1:30. At two in the afternoon we start again. The backs work from 2:00 to 3:00 P.M., the line works from 3:00 to 4:00 P.M., and the ends work from 4:00 to 5:00 P.M. Dinner will be served from 5:30 to 6.00 P.M. At 8:00 P.M., we meet in one unit under the lights for one hour and go through what we have learned in separate groups. This has proven valuable for us.

It is long, hard work for two coaches, but we accomplish much more than we would by trying to work with a large group simultaneously. This method assures us that there will be no boys standing around watching; most of them are busy practically all of the time. We have an opportunity to get personally acquainted with each boy. And each boy gets a fair chance to show what he can do.

It is to the coach's own benefit to have a close look at each prospect. Using this system in early practice, the coach can have a good look at each candidate. Sometimes he will be rewarded with a "find"—a boy who does not possess enough of the outward qualities to warrant a second look, but who may go on to stardom.

Each of these unit practice sessions will be halted ten minutes before the end of the hour or the hour and one-half period so the players may run ten one-hundred yard wind sprints. This is the best criterion I know of to judge the desire of a boy who wants to compete in football. If he is not really a "gutty" football player, he will fold while running these wind sprints. The kids who survive them are in such marvelous physical condition that they are proud of it.

WHAT IS DONE THE FIRST DAY

For approximately three days, we will not suit our varsity players in pads. We will work our new freshmen and new transfers in pads, however, to find out if they have the qualities that we feel are required before they can represent the Lumberjacks.

THE BACKFIELD

The varsity backfield spends much time in the first practices learning and reviewing how to get the ball from the quarterback. We spend hours drilling on this exchange. We feel that the toughest thing to teach is how to get a good hold on the ball and be able to keep possession of it, despite being hit tremendously hard at the line. We run the play patterns that were explained on the blackboard the previous night.

During the first few days, we meet each evening for about thirty minutes. We try to sandwich this meeting between our night meal and our night practice.

We have always started by learning our Red Series first, for no other reason than it is the most natural one to learn. It is the series which includes the old faithful Straight T plays—the dive, the slant, and the end run. These are our bread-and-butter plays, so they are the ones we always start with.

PLAYING A SLOT T BACK IS DIFFERENT

We get many boys from throughout the country, but the majority are from Arizona. They have played under an assortment of offensive formations, but very few have had experience with the Slot T. Only one or two high schools in the state employ this type of offense.

When we get a freshman back who has never played this offense, he is astonished to see how much simpler it is to fathom and how easy it is to learn the plays. Many remark how much easier it seems to get in the open; there does not seem to be as much congestion with the Slot T as there does with the more conventional types of offense.

When the backs are learning their Slot T plays, they generally have only one back to be conscious of, other than the quarterback. Once in a while the slotback will figure into the play pattern, but not often enough to get worried about. From this offense the backs are able to spring into the open in a flash. After we have worked on ball-handling long enough to have everyone handle the ball several times, we switch to other backfield techniques.

The unsung hero on a football team, in my opinion, is the good faking back. Many backs refuse to fake into the line realistically and hard unless the coach is on them constantly. We stress this faking over and over again. We have found it works quite well to have the backs who are faking run so low and so hard that they actually fall; they overbalance themselves forward so much they cannot recover their balance. This is good practice for falling also. They learn to roll on their shoulders as they hit the ground.

Learning to fall is important. If a boy is able to fall properly, his chances of getting hurt are greatly reduced. This drill is fun, too.

We like to have the boys get into groups and stay in these groups for the first few days, so we can get more done. When one group is running a play, one group is huddling, one is coming back from running a play, and two or three are waiting for their turns. We will naturally place our best backs into units that we want them to get used to. In this way, the coaches can watch for mistakes in technique and assignment.

As the backs get the idea of what we want, we will move into pass-protection blocking. We use two different styles for pass-protection blocking when we intend to throw from a pocket. If our backs are able to, they will meet the defensive ends head-on and try to whip them. If, however, our backs are not as large as the defensive ends, they will use another method: They will step up into the line and allow the defensive ends to come in. As the ends pass by, the backs will turn and proceed with them. The quarterback will go a bit deeper when this type of pass protection is being used to force the defensive ends to go deep after him. When the quarterback sees the ends coming in on him, he will stop his backward movement and move forward, toward center. As the ends try to turn, they find that our halfback and fullback are right behind them, forcefully nudging them in the direction they were going and past the quarterback. Using this method, a smaller player can handle a big, rugged specimen. He will use the end's own impetus to get him out of the way.

We drill on both of these types of pass-protection blocking. The boys seem to do better if they are allowed to move from one drill to another after ten or fifteen minutes. The first few days we will conduct these types of drill, always leaving time for each group to run ten 100-yard wind sprints and do fifty push-ups and fifty sit-ups.

Shoe tightness at this time often is a problem. We instruct our boys to take their shoes off the minute they feel a blister developing. Blisters can be avoided in many cases if the boys are permitted to take their shoes home with them in the summer and use them off and on to run in. This toughens their feet.

For any of you who must use old shoes at the start of a season,

I would like to pass on this tip for what it is worth. Have the boy wear his shoes into the shower and get them soaked through and through. Then they will get the impressions of his own feet. I read this suggestion in Cramer's First Aider many years ago, and it saves many blisters.

THE INTERIOR LINEMEN

As the backs are finishing their wind sprints, the interior linemen are loosening up on their own. When the backs have run their last wind sprint, the linemen assemble, ready to go.

We use Crowther's Seven Man Charger blocking sled—a piece of equipment with so many good qualities it is difficult to list them here. It is a prime conditioner, which is important at this early stage.

We form our linemen in a single line in front of the first pad. The first lineman takes an offensive stance, and on the whistle delivers a blow with his right shoulder. He allows the sled to throw him back into position, then hits the second, and so on down the line. As soon as the first blocker clears the first pad, the second man in line will move up and strike it and go right down the line, hitting each of the seven pads, backing off, coming in hard to the next pad.

When they have all hit the sled with the right shoulder, they start at the other end and come back, hitting with the left shoulder. They go through this drill until each boy has hit the sled two times with each shoulder. This really makes the linemen put out.

The drill that I believe has helped us more on this seven-man blocking sled than any other is one we call our "roll out" drill. We use this drill to simulate rolling out of a block. To use the sled effectively for this drill we have a boy hit the first pad with his right shoulder. The sled will throw him back. As he starts back away from the sled he rolls high right shoulder under him, turning his belly to the sky for a split second as he continues to roll a complete turn, staying on his hands and feet as he comes out of the roll. He hits the first pad, rolls out and hits the third, rolls out and hits the fifth, rolls out and hits the seventh. Two times through, using this roll or spin, will tire the boys a bit, too. This drill will do more to help make big, slow men agile than any other drill we know.

We use this same seven-man sled to teach blocking fundamentals. It is heavy enough that one man can't move it, and springy enough so it will not injure the shoulder, as some sleds have been known to do.

If a sled is not available, it is a good idea to use a blocking dummy. A boy must be permitted to get his timing before he is thrown into actual scrimmage; lack of timing will do more to make a boy lose confidence than anything I know. We like to let our boys hit the dummies two or three days before we allow actual contact. We will wait longer than this with the green boy, because we want him to come along slowly.

When we are in a hurry to get a boy into the lineup, it is sometimes necessary to push him faster and harder than we ordinarily would. Our school is quite small in comparison to the larger schools in our state. This limits our turnout of potential football players quite a bit. We therefore lose quite heavily by graduation each year, and this often forces us to use boys with little or no experience. About the only way I know to get a boy ready to compete on a varsity football team is to use him as much as possible. If he is green, he must be taught the things that he is to do by scrimmaging. We will, therefore, scrimmage extensively when we have several green boys in our lineup.

During these first few days, much good can be accomplished by breaking practice up in such a way so each new boy can receive a maximum amount of attention and work. If, for example, we have lost a key tackle or two by graduation or other means, we will spend many hours getting a sophomore or a freshman ready to take his place. In this group work with the linemen, the new boy will be instructed painstakingly, slowly, and deliberately. He will be taught defensive maneuvers first; we have found if we must use a green boy, he can do us more good on defense than he can on offense. If we can get him ready for the defensive platoon, he will be able to spell the regular tackle, at least a little. Offensive work comes harder, but defense seems to be more natural.

We have always had good results teaching our linemen when we have only a few on the field at one time. One coach can supervise the offensive man and one coach can take the defensive man. In this way, much can be accomplished in a short time. After two or three blocks, the offensive player can exchange places with the defensive boy and get two or three shots at defense. With a coach right there to teach him how to work both ways, much more can be accomplished, and in a much shorter time, too.

During the first part of practice in the fall, we like our linemen to go through their assignments at half speed, stressing form. We want them to learn exactly how each type of block is executed. If they exercise proper form in making each block many, many times in slow motion, they will gain the confidence necessary to execute this block in a proper manner when the time comes for them to do it at full speed.

Although we will spend a lot of time at this half-speed blocking, a green boy must get the feeling of competition just as soon as possible. He must be able to react to his opponent's move quickly, and the only way he can learn is to have an opponent come at him full speed. This can be done with the drill shown in Diagrams 145 and 146. We have used this drill for several years and had good results with it.

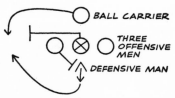

DIAGRAM 145. Full-Speed Blocking Drill.

REACTION DRILL

The reaction drill in Diagram 145 has helped us immeasurably. We place three linemen on offense and one defensive boy head-on the middle lineman. One lineman will act as a back; he holds a ball in his arm and runs to his right at first. The outside lineman will execute a cut-off block on the defensive man, who will fight the pressure.

If the offensive man executes a good block, the defensive man must fight back into the play area. If he is unable to fight through the offensive blocker, he will use the roll-out technique that we have practiced on the seven-man sled: He will back up one step, quickly roll off this block, and fight back into the play. If the back is already on his way upfield and a cut-off maneuver is impossible, the defensive man will sprint at a new angle upfield in his proper pursuit pattern (see Diagram 146).

DIAGRAM 146. Reaction Drill.

Using this drill to both sides of the defensive man helps him acquire quick lateral movement and anticipate pressure quickly. It helps him realize what his correct angle of pursuit is. All that is necessary to teach the inexperienced tackle—or any defensive man, for that matter—the improper technique of pursuit is to allow him to chase the ball-carrier. It soon becomes obvious to the defender that if he is to be successful in stopping the runner, he will have to assume a new angle of pursuit. This angle is determined by the speed of the two boys concerned.

If the runner is faster than the pursuer, the angle will of necessity be sharper; if the defender is as fast or faster than the runner, the angle of pursuit can be less.

The proper angle of pursuit is one of the first things a good defensive man learns. He wants to be in on every tackle, and if he does not assume the correct angle of pursuit he will seldom be in position to help his team.

When we have worked the young (and veteran) players on how to fight pressure, roll out, and pursue, we then have the runner scoot straight at them. The blocker will try to take them to either side or straight back. We work long and hard trying to present the inexperienced player with as many of the possible things he will be faced with in a game. The more familiar he becomes with them before the game, the fewer will be his mistakes in the game itself. These few drills can be of great service to us. They help the offensive personnel execute three blocks—the straight-ahead block, the fill block, and the pulling maneuver used by the Slot T offense so many times. These can all be learned while the defensive player is getting his lesson.

This is just a sample of some of the things we try to do each season during the first few days. We repeat the same things over and over until every one of our linemen has the technique down letter-perfect.

When our first game nears, we want our linemen to be able to execute properly every block we have in our offense. This is not nearly as difficult as it may seem. We only have eight different blocks in our offensive system, and some of them are executed in practically the same way as others, so they are quite easy to learn.

During the practice sessions when we have the squad broken down into small groups, we feel we are able to get a fairly green boy ready for a game if he is willing to pay the price of hard work. Much can be done in small groups that can never be done in large groups.

As we go along, we do the things we find we are weak on.

The days go by so quickly that you wonder where they could have gone. But if you are short-handed, your chances of being ready for a season are usually better.

PRACTICE BY WIDE ENDS

The drills employed to acquaint the wide ends with the types of blocks they will be required to master are few. The first drill will introduce the new end to the procedure of coming back down the line of scrimmage to make a block. This block is the only one that may be completely new to the end; he has probably experienced the other types in his high school playing.

This drill is set up easily: We place an end out about twelve yards from his tackle, and a blocking dummy is set up where the defensive end would be. The holder of the dummy faces the wide end. We like this wide end to execute the cross-body block for his first effort. He will learn to execute this block with his right hip and then his left. If he is six feet tall, he will be able to use all six feet to keep a defensive end from getting in our way. Since his shoulder is only about a third or less of this width, it is much easier for him to make a creditable block with a cross-body effort than it is with a shoulder block. He is much less likely to miss his target.

We teach our men to execute a cross-body block in the following manner: The player will approach his target at almost full speed, which in itself is an advantage over the shoulder block. Just as he gets within arm's length of the defensive man, he simulates throwing a right cross to the chin if he is going to use the right hip. (Be sure the player does not connect with his right cross, or an official may misinterpret the action.)

This action will place his arm across and in front of the intended target. It will force his body in the correct position and whip his hip into the target. Just as the hip is making contact, the right leg will swing in high and behind the target.

As contact is made, the blocker will have one foot on the

ground, and one leg lifted high on the target. It is better to attempt to have both hands across the target's body and on the ground, as the hand not on the ground sometimes falls over the leg of the rival player and may cost the blocker fifteen yards. If both hands are on the ground, they give the blocker better balance—it also keeps the effort from looking like an illegal block.

This drill is repeated many times until the ends have had many turns and been instructed in the proper technique of doing this first and most important block. If they can do a good job on this type of block, they will be of use to the team.

It is a sound idea to instruct the wide ends to wear their hip pads high. This cross-body block often brings painful hip pointers. We have had our share of these pesty things, and our wide ends are the most likely candidates. Every time this has occurred, the trouble is traced to the negligence of the end, who carelessly allowed his hip pads to slip down too far.

When our boys have pretty well mastered this type of block, we teach them the shoulder block in the same manner—that is, with the dummy. When using the shoulder block, it is difficult for the blocker to move into his target at full speed. We have had more success in teaching this type of block by having our blocker move at top speed until he is about four yards from his target. He then spreads his stance and slows to about three-fourths speed. As his stance is spread, it lowers his shoulders and drops his hips low, where they should be. As he slows to about three-fourths speed, he gains better control of himself; he is able to go in either direction with much more agility. With his speed checked and his hips lowered, his head will bull back, his back will be straight, and he will bring his arms up, with his hands on his chest. From this position he is ready to make contact.

We have had much better luck having our blocker head-fake just before making contact. This will often bring the defender's hands and arms up, enabling the blocker to get his shoulder under the defender's hands.

The most common weakness in this type of block is that it is difficult to get the blocker to keep his head up. All blockers have a tendency to drop their eyes to the ground. Place a man just behind the dummy and have him hold his hand up about waist high. After the block, ask the blocker how many fingers the man had showing. A lap around the goal posts (at Arizona State, the coach exercises the right to rap the player on the head with his knuckles, which is worse "punishment" than running) will alert the blocker and aid him in concentrating on keeping his head up, where it belongs.

This wide-end position, over the years, has seen some strange paradoxes. We have had some ends, since we started using the Slot T, who blocked well from out wide with a shoulder block exclusively. We have had others who used the cross-body block almost exclusively. Some have used both. All have done a creditable job.

The finest and the most vicious blocker we ever had at this position was Louis Casillas, one of our famed "Chihuahua Backfield." He used the shoulder very effectively. He would wait in his tracks for the first man on the defensive team to come his way. As he saw the defender coming his way, diagnosing the play, he would cut the man's feet out from under him with a vicious shoulder block that must have rattled his ancestors' bones.

Other excellent blockers from out wide have come back down the line quickly to cut off the wide pursuit before it could get started. If the boy utilizes either block well, we allow him to use whichever is most effective.

During early season practice, dummy blocking can be very important in teaching the boys how we wish the blocks to be executed. If the wide end is a big fellow, he can often be effective by coming back down the line standing straight up and meeting the defensive end face to face. This is a tough block, and the defensive ends would just as soon get hit in another fashion after several of these face-to-face wallops. Big Earl

Randolph was good at this type of block; he stood six feet two and weighed 220 pounds, and when he met an end face to face, the end usually remembered him.

BLOCKING THE LINEBACKER

On one or two plays we will have the wide end hit the line-backer. We make this possible by not having him split as far as usual. He will still execute the blocks just explained. We use this many times when we wish to come to the side away from the slotback. This type of play is shown in Diagram 146a.

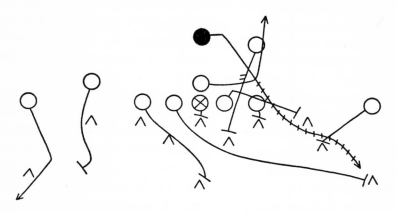

DIAGRAM 146a. Wide End Hitting Linebacker.

About the only other type of block remaining for the wide end is to block the halfback in front of him. We mentioned in an earlier chapter that this block was one reason for using this offense. The end can take as wide a spread as he wishes. The defensive halfback must spread with him a great deal of the time. If the end runs downfield and cuts for the sideline, the defensive halfback must go with him, if the play has any deception. This action alone is often sufficient to serve as a perfect block down-field. If the end can get the defensive half to go with him, the back cannot be up in the line and participating in all the tackles.

When the first few days of practice are over, we expect our

wide ends, our linemen, and our backs to be able to block in the proper manner. This blocking is stressed so much that if a boy cannot block, we will teach him to, or almost die from exhaustion in the attempt. Good blocking is a must at Arizona State College. Without it, any team is a goner.

PASS PATTERNS FOR THE WIDE ENDS

In the chapter on forward passing we mentioned several times the reasons why we feel the Slot T is best suited for moving the ball. We mentioned that, with wide ends as possible aerial targets, a passing attack can help to develop a ball-control offensive with short passes. This is much the same as a Split T team controls the ball with the dive and the option.

In 1957, we played the University of Nevada in Las Vegas. They had a fine youngster of Japanese lineage playing quarterback. He did exactly what I just mentioned, and he presented us with problems. He saw to it that Nevada unleashed a sustained ball-control type of football with a passing attack. He would hit the wide ends, who would drop in their tracks for three yards gain. Then he would strike with the look-in pass. Then he would keep us guessing with the check-out pass. Then the stand-still pass again, where the end would be content to fall forward for two or three yards. We could not keep him from completing these short passes.

We placed a man up tight, head-on the wide end. But the end would fake and be past our boy in a flash. We finally ordered a man to stand in front of the end and throw a cross-body block into him, and we had a man cover him deep after he got to his feet. This worked quite well, until they elected to run the ball. We had practically all our players trying to stop the passing attack. This is a perfect example of the devastation that can be generated by the use of such a flexible attack.

The drills we use in the early part of the season are nothing more than the actual pass patterns we expect our ends to be able to run. We work hard on the cuts and the fakes. These are the two toughest things to teach, in my opinion, but they are indispensable weapons and a must to learn.

In the past, we have drawn pass patterns on the ground with the field limer for realistic and graphic instruction. This is fine, except we don't have enough field space and have to scrimmage over these same lines. Consequently, they become blurred in a hurry. If enough space is available, this is an excellent way to teach footwork, cutting, faking, and the pass patterns themselves.

Just a note before leaving this subject of getting ready for the first game: It is helpful to have your punters and kickoff men do some booting each day. Work on a few kickoff returns at the end of practice during the first few days. This, in itself, serves as a change of pace. If all this is put off until the last moment, costly mistakes may be made on the opening kickoff because the kickoff unit has not had a chance to receive practice on this vital point.

Another thing that is easy for many coaches to put off is the conversion after touchdown. What could actually be of more importance?

A coach must make certain that in his organizational plan he includes time for each of these vital factors. Planning and organization are just as important as blocking and tackling in football—a game that features mental gymnastics to go along with all the physical heroics.

SUMMARY

The organizational plan just presented may seem a bit strenuous, but it is the only way I know for an undermanned staff to get a team ready to compete on equal terms with clubs that have twice as much coaching help.

Breaking the team into small groups is the best method for a coach to get personally acquainted with the abilities of each boy. He can see for himself what the boy can and cannot do.

He will have a chance to make wiser decisions on cutting his squad. His inexperienced boys can obtain that vital personal tutoring that is so necessary to get them ready. I have found that with this personal tutoring a player can gain the valuable experience needed in approximately half the time normally required.

What makes a player a good player? Usually he is a capable performer if he knows what is going on. It is possible to get a boy to the point where he will make very few mistakes by giving him personalized attention early in the season. When coaching help is limited, sessions with small groups is the only method of giving personalized attention.

CHAPTER THIRTEEN

Scouting for the Slot T

In small colleges and in high schools, we have a problem in scouting that is not found in larger schools: the problem of the one-man scouting force. How much information can one man be expected to bring us? Generally, he will not be able to gather a great assortment of information; we have a simplified scouting sheet for him to use. But although the information he seeks is not great in amount, it is great in value, as far as the Slot T is concerned.

WHAT DOES HE LOOK FOR?

During the warm-up period, the scout will observe the punters to determine who seems to be the top kicker. When the game starts, he will make certain that the boy who was kicking the ball then is actually the man who does the punting. Many times the boy who kicks the ball a country mile in warmup will not be the punter in the game. The same is true for the kickoff man. It is important to be able to tell our receivers approximately where to line up to catch the kickoff and punts, also.

A team can get in a hole at the start of the game by not having its kickoff or punt receivers deep enough. If the ball goes over the head of the receiver, we have lost any chance of a return. Ball games are difficult enough to win with all the breaks, so why let an important thing like this go unnoticed?

Our scout will check on whether the punter is right-footed or left-footed. How many steps does he take to get the ball off? This will often help to set up a punt-blocking stunt. If the punter is slow, or if he takes too many steps and gets himself too close to the line, our chances of blocking the punt are good. This is the information the scout can get before the game starts. He can check these findings throughout the game to see that they are still correct.

The scout will note who the best passers are and who the best pass catchers seem to be. He will look for any left-handed passers. Many teams will use a left-handed passer at the right halfback position and throw a reverse pass with him running to his left. This can be a dangerous pass if it catches the defense asleep. The scout will check the passer while he is warming up to see if he is accurate. Can he throw accurately long and short? Does he throw on the run? Does he roll out to throw? Does he roll out and stop to throw? The defensive ends on our team will be greatly assisted if they know the quarterback stops on a roll-out. They will be able to rush harder, instead of pedaling to the sidelines with the roll-out motion. Check these things against what actually happens in the game. The most important item to check is whether the passer panics under rushing pressure.

If our scout is able to tell us these few things accurately, we can make certain definite plans. We can take the fullest possible advantage of all information our scout brings back. Any one of these things mentioned above can be vital in a close game. A blocked punt has won many a game. A reverse pass has caught many defensive halfbacks sleeping. A long, booming punt has gone over the heads of many safety men and resulted in the team starting out in the hole. If a team has no opportunity to return a punt or a kickoff, the kicking team may have placed their opponents in a hole from which they can never recover.

In the few minutes before a game, our scout can get all this information with no hurry and no great pressure. He can watch from his press-box seat and obtain a great amount of valuable information before the game has ever started.

On the kickoff, we want our scout to notice these things:

1. Who is the first man downfield under the kickoff?
2. Who is staying back playing the safety against returns?
3. Are the ends coming down playing their position—that is, are they protecting the outside?

With this bit of information, we have an important advantage. If, for example, there are one or two men who are far ahead of their teammates, we can make a big hole through which to re-

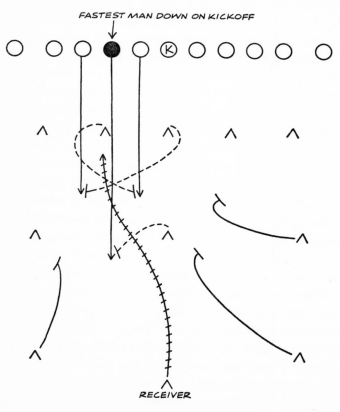

DIAGRAM 147. Kickoff Return.

turn the kickoff by eliminating the player who is ahead of his teammates. We will assign a blocker to this first man downfield. He will not knock him down, but will turn and go with the fast man, staying just behind him. As the lead man tries to go for the ball-carrier, our blocker will force him on up the field in the direction he was running. We will force the hole behind this fast man by executing a cross-block on the two men to either side of him. This kickoff return is shown in Diagram 147.

A kickoff return that employs the same principle can be used against a team that has the habit of leaving the same person back to protect against runbacks on the kickoff. If his teammates fail to fill the gap that opens when this man stops to

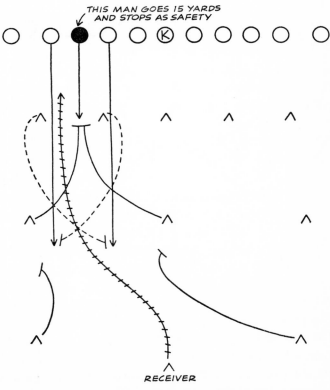

DIAGRAM 148.   Kickoff Return.

protect, there will be a hole between the two men to either side of him. Using this bit of information, the return shown in Diagram 148 can be profitable.

If the ends coming down under the kickoff are not conscious of protecting the outside, we have a special return to take advantage of this type of deficiency. Shown in Diagram 149 is the kickoff return that we use for this situation.

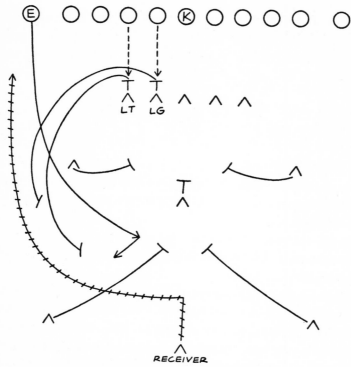

DIAGRAM 149.   Kickoff Return.

We will set the end up by faking a return right up the center. All the backs will get in front of the ball-carrier, who will go as far as he can up the middle. When he sees that he has reached the limit, he will swing out to the sideline. If the return is planned to our left, the left tackle and the left guard will block, passively, the men coming downfield in their area. They will then loop out

to the sideline and make the key block on the defensive end
when he tries to recover and protect the flank after he has found
himself out of position.

These three things may seem unimportant, but they have paid
great dividends for us over the years.

AFTER THE GAME STARTS

When the game starts, our scout will busy himself finding a
few important weaknesses for our Slot T to go to work on. It
is easily done, because the Slot T is so versatile it can take advantage of almost anything. After the kickoff, when our foes
are on defense, our scout will look for these things:

1. How do the deep backs adjust to flankers?
2. Do they rotate to a flanker?
3. Does the defense cover a wing set-up the same way they
   do a flanker set-up?

If we can obtain this information, we can prepare an intelligent
offensive plan to capitalize on. Here is how we attempt to obtain
this information:

We have already explained the terms used to describe our
offensive formations: flanker right, flanker left, wing right, wing
left, and split formation.

Our scout will note what position the offense is in and, with
the first letters of our own formation nomenclature, he will describe their formation. For example, "FR" will indicate to us
that on this play the offense was in a similar alignment to our
flanker right formation. The "FL" will indicate that the offense
was aligned in an alignment similar to our own flanker left
formation.

These letters are important because they will indicate how
the defense adjusts to each offensive pattern. Our scout will make
a note of this. When the defensive backfield has three deep backs,
we refer to this alignment as a diamond. The scout will indicate
this defensive alignment with a little rafter indicating the top

part of a diamond, like this: $\wedge$. If the defense has two deep backs, we call this alignment a box. The scout will indicate this by drawing the top half of a box, like this: $\sqcap$.

With these simple notations, the scout can record a running account of the game. He will note that the offensive team is in a flanker right formation and that the defense had three deep backs to counter this particular formation. If the right half carries the ball through the guard hole, he will use our number system and write "22." This will indicate that the two back carried through two hole. He will make the following marks to record this valuable bit of information: "FR- $\wedge$ 22." On the following play, the offensive team may come in with a straight T. The scout will note this by making the letter "T." He will follow this T with a diamond or a box, depending upon how the defense reacted to this particular formation: "T $\wedge$ 23," or "T $\sqcap$ 23."

The next thing the scout will look for on each play is any weakness in the defensive personnel. If one of the backs is more than eight yards deep or if one of them is less than seven yards deep when they are in a diamond defense, it is noted: The letters "FR" and the diamond or box are followed, for example, by "LH9" if the left half is deep or "LH6" if the left half is too tight. Do the halfbacks come up very fast? This will be noted once in a while. Are the halfbacks deep-conscious? Do they really zoom in and break up a hook pass? These things will be noted during a time-out. And so forth.

When and if the defense uses the two-deep set-up with four linebackers, or a "five-four-two" defense, the scout will check the inside linebackers. Are they really tough when the play comes straight at them? Do they whip a blocker, or try to go around him? These things will be checked mentally, but written down only during time out. Are the outside linebackers pass-conscious? Do they move up on their first move? Do they commit themselves quickly? Would a reverse catch them out of position?

DIAGNOSING THE DEFENSE

The simplest method we know of to determine quickly a defensive alignment is to count the deep backs and the linebackers, then subtract from eleven. If there are three deep backs and two linebackers, the defense will be some kind of six-man line. We refer to this alignment as even. If there are three deep backs and one linebacker, this will tell us that the defense is a seven-man line.

This is important when the team we are to play is in trouble. Inside their ten-yard line, what defense do they use? The actual alignment of the line is not too important, because this can vary easily from one week to another. It is much more difficult to change the pattern of the deep backs from one week to another. For this reason, we concentrate our attention upon the things that we feel will be static from one week to the next.

Our scout will notice any extremely hard-charging linemen. Can they be trapped? He will also take note of a "patsy" along the line, if there seems to be one. This is sometimes difficult to determine, because the scout may know nothing of the relative strengths of the two men facing each other. If one is the best blocker in the country, he may make even a good player look bad. Habits, such as a tremendous charge, are more valuable to know. It is difficult for a person to be a tremendously hard-charger and still be able to play soft and hand-fight. The scout will take note of how the ends play. Do they play soft? Or do they crash hard and shallow? This information concerning the line can help our Slot T get under way.

HOW IS THIS INFORMATION USED?

Let us go over this information together. When the scout returns, he will make a neat chart of his findings, and we will go over it.

The first thing we want to know is anything that the scout feels will take advantage of a particular weakness he has noted. How can we score in the quickest and easiest fashion? This is where the scouting report comes to life. Is there a man on the defensive backfield unit who commits himself too quickly? Do any of the deep backs leave their territory and go with the flow of the play? If this is the case, a fake wide-end run with a check-out pattern, as shown in Diagram 150, can result in a touch-down, or at least a long gainer.

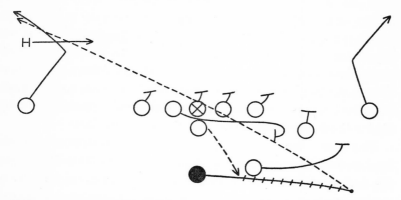

DIAGRAM 150.   Fake Wide End Run with Fake Check Out Pattern.

We have found many times that if we are successful on the first play, it gives our team the added boost that is needed to start moving. The impetus built up from this first successful play can often carry through the whole game. When two evenly-matched teams meet, a slight advantage at the start of the game is often the deciding factor in the eventual outcome.

On the basis of what the scout has learned, we can now go to work attacking the positions that he found may be vulnerable. If, for example, the halfbacks on a three-deep defense play too far back, we can start by throwing hook passes and hook-and-in-the-hole passes like the one shown in Diagram 151.

These two patterns alone, mixed with regular running plays, can keep an offense moving. They also set up a possible scoring

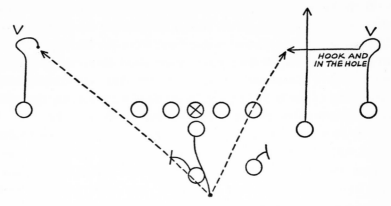

DIAGRAM 151.   Hook-and-in-the-Hole Passes.

play if the halfbacks get too determined to stop these hook passes. The most dangerous play in football is the hook-and-go pass. It is a terrific pass to use against halfbacks who are trying to stop the hook passes too aggressively.

This pass, shown in Diagram 152, can really be a problem for the defense when thrown from the Slot T. This is because the end is spread wide and the defensive half is usually trying to cover him by himself. If the defensive man makes a mistake, there is usually no one there to help him.

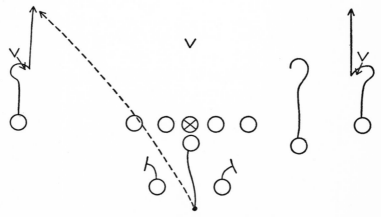

DIAGRAM 152.   Hook Pass from Slot T.

If the ends crash tough and shallow, we can almost disregard them. Our wide ends on the Slot T offense are in good position to keep anyone on the defensive team from rushing straight out to the flat. If we can keep the defense away from the short flat, we can gain consistently enough on our end runs to maintain possession of the ball. (By the "short flat" we mean an area outside the defensive end and four or five yards deep.)

The Slot T has a "permanent" wide end posted ten or twelve yards wide. When the play begins, he will start back toward his teammates. A hard-charging defensive end will eliminate himself from a wide-end run. Therefore, our wide end will look for a linebacker covering the short flat for the end. If we can wipe him out, our interference will be in front of the ball-carrier and in a position to take care of upcoming halfbacks and safety men.

When the report indicates the end will play what is referred to as a "boxing end," or an end that moves two yards across the line, we will concentrate our attack inside this end. We will block from the inside out with one of our linemen and send a back or another lineman through the hole to get the linebacker. These two types of end play are shown in Diagrams 153 and 154.

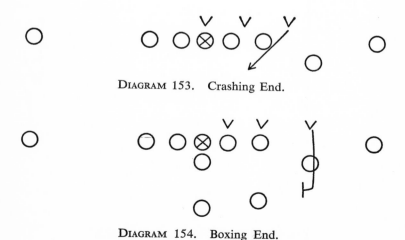

DIAGRAM 153. Crashing End.

DIAGRAM 154. Boxing End.

Usually if an end is moving straight upfield, as he will do when he is playing the boxing-end type of defense, a linebacker will have the inside responsibility. It is difficult to run outside this type of defensive end. We have had better luck blocking out on this type of defensive end, using our guard. We will shoot the onside halfback up through the hole after the linebacker. Occasionally a change of pace is successful, with the halfback and the guard changing assignments. These two types of blocks are shown in Diagrams 155 and 156; both are used against a defensive end who is boxing us in.

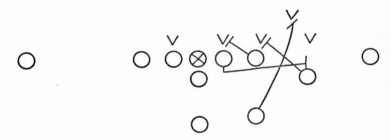

DIAGRAM 155.   Halfback On Linebacker.

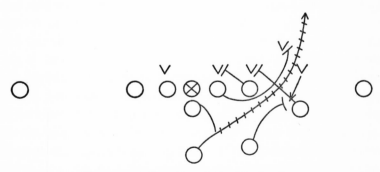

DIAGRAM 156.   Guard On Linebacker.

The linebacker's style of play is one of the most important things our scout looks for. If linebackers are too tight to the line, they have a difficult time covering on quick passes to either side of them and on end runs. Linebackers get themselves all tangled up in the feet of their own linemen when trying to move laterally after they make the mistake of getting too close up. If they play too loose or too far away from the line, it is sometimes possible to move the ball straight at the linebackers.

These few items of information are not difficult to obtain. Of course, this information is not nearly as complete as two- or three-man staffs can get, but we have had some success with a one-man scouting staff. Usually one or two areas will be found vulnerable. If we cannot find a weakness somewhere on their team, we will have a long and rugged afternoon ahead of us.

An important defensive point for the scout to note is whether or not we can trap someone along the line. If the defense is really bearing in at one spot or another, it is possible to trap on the Slot T effectively—and, if we can get through the line on a trap play, that our chances of a long gainer are good. The defense is so spread out that all that is needed to do is wipe out the one linebacker moving into the hole with the fake.

This is approximately all we will concern our scout with while our future opponent is on defense. As soon as they get the ball, we have our scout watch for more information.

The first question, naturally, is what offensive system is used by this team? Do they run from a Straight T, a Single Wing, a Split T? Do they throw the ball a great deal? If so, who are their prime receivers? It is difficult for one man to check all the receivers' patterns, but he will be able to find the preferred receiver most of the time. He will also try to figure how they plan to free this choice receiver. Some teams will flood a zone to get the best receiver free. Others will widen their choice receiver twelve to fifteen yards and try to force the defense into covering him with one man.

If they can get the defense to do this, and if their receiver is a good faker with adequate speed, he may be able to outwit the defensive man and free himself for a touchdown pass or a long gainer. If the latter plan is used (even though the offense does spread an end out so wide we are forced to cover him man-for-man or one-on-one), we will know this. We will place our finest defensive man on their top receiver. We will also plan to give him some help in the form of linebackers or safety men. Against this type of plan, a loose linebacker can sometimes be of help covering inside and short of the widespread end, leaving the deep halfback with only deep responsibility. See Diagram 157.

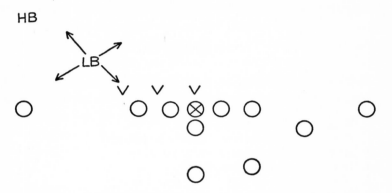

DIAGRAM 157.   Defense Against Spread Receivers.

As we mentioned earlier, it is nearly impossible to discern whether an offensive lineman is really a great blocker or whether the defensive man in front of him is a "patsy."

If we can find the offensive pattern of calling plays, many times this will help. This is especially true early in the game. If they run their plays in sequence, for example, they will dive a halfback on first down of the game. They will slant their fullback off tackle following this, and they will pitch out to their halfback the third play. Some teams will do this early in a game. It is early in a game when stopping the opponents can be helpful in making them unsure of themselves. If we can make a team unsure of the things that they have a lot of faith in, we have an excellent chance of defeating them. True, all teams don't discourage this easily, but some do. Some individuals on the opponents' team may discourage easily. Our boys will listen for grumblers along the line, and we will try to run the ball over grumblers when we go on the offensive again.

In planning a defense for a game, we have been successful several times in stunting from some of the weirdest defenses one ever dreamed of. Especially is this true if we feel that we are going to be outmanned. If a team fails to gain or loses ground on several consecutive plays, it is possible to get them wrangling among themselves, and this dissension will defeat many teams.

SUMMARY

If the scout can bring us the following information about the offense of the team we are preparing to meet, we will be satisfied:

1. What is their offensive system?
2. Are they predominantly runners or passers?
3. Who is their bread-and-butter back?
4. Who is their choice receiver?
5. What patterns do they like to free him on?
6. What hole on the line will they run through when short, hard yardage is need?
7. How do they use flankers? (This is usually covered in the beginning, when the offensive system is explained.)
8. Is their quarterback tall or short?
9. Does he throw from a pocket or roll out? This is especially important if the quarterback is small and a pocket passer. In such cases, the moment a pass is smelled our linemen will rush high with their arms outstretched. This makes it difficult for a short passer to find his receivers.

These few pieces of information are not difficult to obtain, but they are important if we expect to be able to defend against this team intelligently.

With the one-man scouting system that is so common among the small schools, we can only get a limited amount of information. If this information is exactly what a coach wants, however, intelligent use can be made of it.

CHAPTER FOURTEEN

A Coach and the Press

Let's face it: A coach who is poor in public relations and who, through his own fault, receives a "bad press" could be on the way to the poor house. His future is none too rosy.

I can't emphasize enough the importance of having a good working relationship with the press. True, it calls for understanding between the coach and newsmen. But a high-level relationship is a must. Some coaches feel that this is just as important as blocking and tackling—and I'm inclined to agree.

To put it mildly, a coach is a harassed individual. Besides keeping his football players on friendly terms, he must also develop the same relationship with the faculty, fans, and booster groups, and who knows who else. Adding to this list, newsmen —people who are vitally important to your program—should be no bother at all. In fact, you should look forward to good public relations.

A coach's successful press relations hinge on a familiar word in football—organization. A coach should attempt to set up some ground rules, so that members of the press can understand his problems and he can understand theirs. When I speak of newsmen, of course, I refer to members of all the news media, including radio and television.

Most high school coaches are not too troubled with wholesale invasions of sportswriters and sportscasters into dressing rooms. They usually have to deal with only one or two newsmen, and relationships such as these most often are close and agreeable.

But on the college level, some problems begin to develop. The smaller colleges are often in the same position as high schools—one or two newsmen to deal with, and no more—and consequently they should have few problems. But the larger colleges and universities offer challenges. Many of these schools are in or near metropolitan areas. This means dealing with sportswriters and columnists from two or more papers and sportscasters from several radio and TV stations. A coach of a larger school must deal with from five to thirty newsmen, often on a daily basis, during the season. And this is where organization is needed.

Naturally, the larger colleges and universities have sports publicists to help take pressure off the coach. But a firm line of agreement and organization is needed between the coach and his sports publicist to keep matters in hand. You will note that I said "firm," and that is exactly what I mean.

The coach must let his press representative know exactly what hours of the day he feels he will be available to the press and what hours he wishes to be left undisturbed to take care of the many other duties that face a coach throughout his busy day.

But a word of caution here: A coach is derelict in his duty if he doesn't understand that some newspapers are morning papers, some evening. Usually these writers have different working hours and different press deadlines. It is best to find out when it will be convenient for these writers to talk to you and see if they can be worked into your schedule. If they can, so much the better. If not, the writers, like football coaches, must learn to be flexible. But understanding does help—on both sides.

ALTERNATE NEWS RELEASES

The same understanding is called for when news releases— stories pertaining to you or your team or school—are announced.

Be sure to alternate the releases, first one in time for the afternoon-paper deadline, then the next one for the morning-paper deadline. Radio and television usually go along with the alternate releases.

Coaches of smaller schools who are not endowed with sports publicists and who do not have funds for football brochures can do much to make smooth relations with the press. See to it that your hometown newspaper, radio station and television station receive typewritten rosters of your squad, with all pertinent information, including uniform numbers. Include correct phonetic pronunciation clues for names that are difficult to pronounce; it's a real distraction during a newscast to hear a sportscaster mispronounce a football player's name. Your local sports editor will be grateful if you double-space all your releases, type on only one side of the paper, and use wide margins.

A smaller school coach would be wise to search for a sports-minded journalism student in his institution. With only a bit of training, this youngster can be your "publicist," sending out news releases, rosters, and so forth. If you can find a conscientious student, your press problems for the season will be solved.

One headache for almost all coaches is the incessant demand for photos of players. This is especially true in the larger schools. I have found that a picture day, usually the day preceding the first actual day of practice, is the best way to get most of the photos out of the way. Naturally, more requests for photos will be made as the season progresses, especially if the team or an individual player is having a spectacular season. But this is a problem all coaches face, so make the best of it.

COOLING-OFF PERIOD

Organization is extremely important on the day of the game. A coach must decide what latitude he wishes to show in the dressing room after the game. Most coaches feel that a ten-, fifteen-, or twenty-minute "cooling off" period is desirable immediately after a game before newsmen are allowed into dressing rooms for their after-game stories. This obviously will save you embarrassing statements, especially if the fortunes of war did not go your way in a close game.

If you do make such a rule, see that it is enforced all through the season. Most newsmen will understand the reason for this "cooling off" period, although some of them with pressing deadlines will want to get their stories as soon as possible. And who can blame them? They have a job to do, and the conscientious newsman will do his best to get his story.

Some coaches feel that newsmen should be banned from talking to players and quoting them. Other coaches find this is not too objectionable, if the newsmen show some prudence. This boils down to the fact that if you trust a newsman, or if you know he is on friendly terms, you can usually allow him the run of the dressing room after a game.

Unfortunately, as most coaches in metropolitan areas find out sooner or later, a newsman comes along who is not too friendly, or who is puffed up by the importance of his position. (This rarely happens in smaller towns.) Such a newsman can hurt a coach, his players, and the school. This can be embarrassing if it persists, and restrictions may be needed. It is difficult to ban a newsman from talking to the various players, but you can tell your players that all comments must be cleared either with a coach or the sports publicist to avoid embarrassing statements.

If you are constantly bothered by a troublemaker, a letter or personal visit to his publisher or station president should clear the air. I advise this only as a last resort. But I am told by those who have feen forced to use this weapon that it does get results.

Nothing can irritate a president of a school more than irresponsible statements attributed to a coach or a player. And, once again, you cannot blame the president, for he is the head of an academic institution that demands common sense and high values from students and faculty members alike.

NEWSMEN ARE HUMAN

The troublemakers in the press world are few. I, personally, have not had trouble with a newsman yet, and I consider myself lucky.

I try to visualize a newsman's problems—and he has them, just as you and I do. I am happy to say that several newsmen are among my best friends.

Because of this close relationship with newsmen, I have found that these so-called "hard-boiled" members of the fourth estate are no more crusty than anyone else. They are human beings, and if they are mistreated by a coach, they react like most human beings: They resent it. If the mistreatment gets serious enough, the newsman will find a way to strike back, and he is in a powerful position to turn the public against a coach by innuendoes, comments in his newspaper or over the air, and so forth.

A coach can find that matters usually just roll along at a normal pace if he is on friendly terms with the press. But the tide turns in a hurry if one or more newsmen are suddenly your "enemies" instead of your friends.

I hope I have painted a picture here that you will try to remember; it is more than important to realize that these factors are necessary in the over-all makeup of a successful coach.

One of the most cogent stories involving a coach and his relations with the press was told to me several years ago. It is a short, simple story, yet it serves as a most glaring example of the wrong attitude on the part of a coach.

A high school coach in a small town was in a position where the sports editor of the tiny daily newspaper had to rely on him to call in the results of the game on road trips. One night after a game on the road the sports editor failed to receive his call from the coach. It later developed that the coach had lost, and therefore did not feel like calling in the results of the game. The editor was forced to call the rival coach and barely had time to get a few details of the game into the paper that night.

The coach won his next road game and happily called in the results. But the third road game again saw the coach go down to defeat—and again, there was no phone call. The editor finally saw the light and blistered the coach in print. Townspeople came to know the coach as a poor loser, and at the end of the school term he was released from his duties.

This story is analogous to life in general, and not merely the trials and tribulations of the coaching profession. Persons in all walks of life are "winners" and "losers" in their daily business dealings. The coach is no different. Show me the person who can lose and bounce back with a smile and keep on trying, and you show me a person who will succeed much more often than the poor loser.

Often I hear about the terrible problems confronting a football coach. Some coaches—too many, in my opinion—continually cry about these problems. If it isn't the school's president, it's the alumni, or the star tackle, or a nosy newsman who is the troublemaker.

I like to look at it in this light: When I went into coaching, I realized these problems existed. I accepted the challenge along with the others that I shouldered. We ask our football players to be both mentally and physically tough; I see no reason for a football coach to be any different.

SUMMARY

To summarize, let me point out that truth is the greatest weapon working in your favor when you deal with newsmen. Do not try to lie or be evasive; you can be hurt badly. If you feel that it is in the best interests of the team to leave out some practice details as an important game approaches, the newsman will honor this request if you "level" with him at all times.

And if you are the type of coach who believes in team prayer before and after a game, as I do, make it a point to close this ceremony to the press, and especially to photographers. Photos of prayer meetings, to me, seem in poor taste; prayers should be recited quietly and peacefully. Newsmen will not object to this request.

Another important item: If you are asked to appear on a television program, try to find out what kind of advertiser is sponsoring the program. Often a beer company will sponsor sports programs. I have no objection, myself, to appearing on a program with such a sponsor (although I am an abstainer), but this could be embarrassing to the school president or the athletic director. It is always prudent to know about these things before you commit yourself. (A conscientious TV sportscaster or radio man will usually notify you in advance.)

And here's something that should be taken into consideration. Newsmen are usually qualified football followers, but some are not among the keenest students of football in the world. If you realize this, try to help them along. This patience will pay off in the long run.

Good organization is the key to good relations with members of news media. The many facets of this coach-newsmen relationship could never be covered in just one chapter, but if the coach has taken enough precautions in his original organizing, he will find that most problems take care of themselves. And this includes the problems of coordinating and disseminating news from the many people involved in a football operation, so the left hand knows what the right hand is saying. A disorganized effort, with different versions of the same story coming from different people on the coaching staff or elsewhere in the school, is one of the worst things that could happen.

Most of these potential trouble spots, as you probably surmised, can be caused by poor preparation. The key is *organization,* and a coach willing to spend the time to get his press affairs in order will never regret it.

CHAPTER FIFTEEN

Psychology and Burning Pride

"Through this door pass the toughest football players alive.*"
This is the message that greets our players when they enter our dressing-room door. You could almost call it our team's creed.

This is part of the psychology that has been tremendously important in helping us achieve the success we have enjoyed at Arizona State. In my opinion, psychology is one of the most important factors in coaching the game. Our Slot T offensive system has given us a real advantage over our opponents, but a little use of psychology here and there has helped us to get a few extra miles out of our boys, too!

Being able to handle football players requires use of a vast reservoir of psychology, as any coach can attest. Why is it that we so often see a coach lose his job because of a poor record, then see his replacement take over and win with virtually the same material? The answer often lies in the proper use of psychology, which tops the list of requirements for conducting a successful football program.

But before any type of psychology can work, a coach must treat his job as a labor of love. He must enjoy and appreciate working with youngsters, or he is doomed. "Building character" is the most facetious term in football today, but psychology can help build character, believe it or not.

The feeling of belonging is especially important. The *esprit de corps* of the U.S. Marine Corps Raiders is a wonderful example of one successful psychological method that gives a group of boys fantastic pride in belonging to a team.

They made it so rugged to be a Raider that only the tough survived. It was that simple.

We use the same system to help build pride in our team: We make it so tough to be a Lumberjack that those who survive the ordeal are justifiably proud of themselves.

The players see so many candidates drop out in our elimination drills that those who stay with us know they are men. They realize they belong to a team to which not just anyone can belong. The pride generated almost puts the team "in orbit" right then and there.

Our freshmen are never allowed to pass through the dressing-room door with our "toughest" sign adorning it until they have been accepted as members of our team. They must be regarded as worthy Lumberjacks before they rise to this honor. And make no mistake—they consider it an honor.

Here's an example of how seriously our boys believe in the sign and what it stands for. At one practice session, a player fell down on these high standards. His actions were almost shameful in the eyes of coaches and players alike; he was scolded, and even his courage was doubted. When we came in at the end of practice, one of his teammates had placed the player's gear outside the door where the sign is posted.

Needless to say, our "problem child" rose to spectacular heights after that. Actually, of course, we rarely have to resort to such measures, but this does indicate how our "creed" affects our players.

Another pride-provoking slogan at Arizona State College is: "Anyone can play when he is well; it takes a *man* to play when he is hurt."

Our football players take great pride in living up to this motto. On occasion, a player will be on the ground, gasping for breath after a blow in the belly, or possibly shaken up. His teammates will gather around, teasing him, "Come on, get up, Joe. Anyone can play when he is well; it takes a man to play when he is hurt!" Or it might be: "A Lumberjack is never on the ground. Get up before someone steps on you!"

It goes without saying that we are always alert to the possibility of serious injury. But the minor, bothersome injuries seem to evaporate into the air with this type of attitude.

The Lumberjacks will tease a teammate to oblivion and back if he limps on anything short of a broken leg. The spirit is fabulous, and here is proof: In five years at Arizona State, I have never seen a player carried off the field. Some possibly should have been, but they refused to allow themselves the distinction of being the first.

We talk a great deal about the importance of being proud of what we are. How can we be proud if we are not as good as we can be? This question is of concern to both teams and individuals.

We have youngsters representing several different races and minority groups on our teams. Our team members try to represent their factions in the best possible way; they always strive to reflect credit on their group.

To me, a most interesting aspect of football psychology is getting each boy to perform to the best of his ability. This is where psychology comes into its own—in handling each boy a bit differently to get 150 percent effort out of him.

It is necessary to praise some boys. It is necessary to yell at others. Still others need only to be left alone. Some will need a combination of the two. This is where the great game of human relations begins to get interesting. How much can a boy take? Better find out before you reach that point.

Discipline is another challenge. Have you ever noticed how differently boys react to discipline? Some take it in stride. Others swell up like a toad.

What is said at critical times will often determine whether a boy stays on the team or is asked to turn in his suit. If proper psychology is used, such painful requests need not be made.

A coach can sense when a youngster has had about all he can stomach. We each have a saturation point. It is a good idea to stop before the boy reaches this critical point.

CHAPTER SIXTEEN

The Intrinsic Values of Football

This book is largely devoted to what coaches and players put into the game of football. What do they get out of it?

First of all, a college education that would otherwise be impossible or achieved with much difficulty is a reward for many players. I have played with and talked to many prominent citizens who admitted that if it had not been for football, they would have had no higher education.

Second, in few other endeavors, and in no other sport can a youth experience more life-like situations than on the friendly battlefield of football. There are many circumstances and problems associated with the game that closely parallel those of life.

How far in life can a man go who refuses to cooperate? If he is a misfit, he will never get a chance to prove his maximum skill in the profession of his choice. Football teaches that cooperation is the only method by which one can succeed.

And how about loyalty? A man will rarely, if ever, get to the top if he does not have this trait. Football players learn the true meaning of the word. They live and play with people who are loyal to each other, their coach, and their school. There is great carry-over value in later life.

A player is also educated in the good, old-fashioned school of hard knocks. A person who hasn't experienced the sensation of losing hasn't lived. Players learn that they will win sometimes and lose at other times, and that they must control their emotions after defeat no matter how much they wanted to win. They learn to work harder after defeat. Most important, they learn that through cooperation, hard work, and loyalty, victories will outnumber defeats.

Democracy at its best can be found on the football field. A player is not judged by who his father is, by his religious beliefs, or by the fact that he may be a member of a minority group. All men are equal on the field; each performs and is rewarded according to his abilities.

As for the coach, his satisfaction lies in the growth of his players and what the game has done for them. His chief reward is the knowledge that he has helped them toward maturity. And in the long run, his performance is measured by how well he has helped equip his players to achieve a meaningful life.

Index

A

Ability, utilization of limited amount of, 32-33
Adjustment of defense, continual, as destructive factor, 82
Alvarey, Al, 131
Angles, utilization of in planning blocks, 43-44
Arizona State, 47:
   and slot T formation (*see* Slot T)
   method of for receiving ball from center, 69-71
   players' attitude towards, 136
   use of player psychology at, 177, 178, 179
Arizona, University of, 16, 40
Association learning, 59
Automatics, calling of, 86-87

B

Backfield patterns, series method of teaching (*see also* Series plays):
   advantage of, 14
   Blue Series, 12-14
   Red Series, 7, 8
   White Series, 7, 9-11
Backs (*see also* Fullback; Halfback; Quarterback; Slotback):
   numbering of in Slot T formation, 5-6
   responsibility of in setting up defensive halfback for tackle's block, 48
   teaching of backfield patterns to, 7-14

Ball, the:
   exchange of, 71
   handling of by center, 41
   receiving of from center, 69-71
   snapping of, 41-42
     by center, 39-40
   use of in drill, 49
Bisbee (Arizona) High School, 3
Blackboard, use of in teaching series plays, 80
   by fullback, 23
   by guards and tackles, *compared*, 48
   by lunge charge, 45
   by medium-sized player, 43
   calling of assignment of by quarterback, 47
   execution of lead block by tackle for post block by guard, 49
   for dive play, 92-93
   for wide end run, 54-55
   importance of for slotback, 27
   inside-out, 9
   in straight T formation, 4
   methods of for opening off-tackle holes, 53
   of defensive halfback, by tackle, 48
   rules of
     for centers, 62, 63-64
     for guards, 62-63
     for slotbacks, 64-65
     for wide ends, 65
     for play off tackle, 59-60
     for fake-block, 60
     terminology, *defined*, 61-62
   straight-ahead, by guard, 44-45